AGRICULTURAL DEVELOPMENT IN JAPAN

THE LAND IMPROVEMENT DISTRICT
IN CONCEPT AND PRACTICE

by

GIL LATZ

PORTLAND STATE UNIVERSITY

UNIVERSITY OF CHICAGO

GEOGRAPHY RESEARCH PAPER NO. 225

1989

Library of Congress Cataloging-in-Publication Data

Latz, Gil, 1952-
Agricultural development in Japan.

(Geography research paper ; no. 225)
Bibliography: p. 105.
Includes index.
1.   Reclamation of land--Japan--Saitama-ken--History.
2.   Water-supply, Agricultural--Japan--Saitama-ken--
History.   3.   Irrigation districts--Japan--Saitama-ken--
History.   4.   Saitama-ken (Japan)--History.
I. Title. II. Series: Geography research paper (Chicago,
Ill.) ; no. 225.
HD1741.J32S254   1989   333.76'0952   89-943
ISBN   0-89065-129-9

Geography Research Papers are available from:

The University of Chicago

Committee on Geographical Studies

5828 South University Avenue

Chicago, Illinois 60637-1583

CONTENTS

CONTENTS

CHARTS

FIGURES

TABLES

v

MAPS

ACKNOWLEDGMENTS

The road to and from Japan is a long one. Physical distances are great and cultural differences are pronounced. It is the fortunate traveler indeed who can recount, as I can, the many people who guided his research and made substantial contributions to it.

At the University of Chicago I would like to acknowledge intellectual and financial support from the Department of Geography and the Division of the Social Sciences (1976-79), as well as from the Center for Far Eastern Studies (1979-80). I am indebted in particular to two professors of the Geography Department, Norton Ginsburg and Paul Wheatley, for sharing with me their profound cultural and socioeconomic grasp of Asian societies. Norton Ginsburg steadfastly supported the research project with sage advice and deserves special recognition for sparking my initial interest in the field of geography. It was under his tutelage that I acquired the skills needed to conduct research on Japanese society. The creative enthusiasm of fellow geography graduate students also had a formative influence on my intellectual development.

At the University of Tokyo, where I was a research student, *kenkyūsei*, from 1980 to 1983, I wish to acknowledge intellectual support from the Institute of Human Geography. Participation in the institute's graduate student seminar and other courses granted a unique perspective on the characteristics of agricultural development in Japan. Professor and Chair Nishikawa Osamu made a number of substantive contributions to the research project. In addition, he graciously introduced me to other faculty in the university and officials at the Ministry of Agriculture, and guided me in the field during the course of data collection. I would also like to acknowledge Professor Yamaguchi Takashi for his assistance.

Nearly all members of the institute contributed to the research effort, but special mention should be made of two research associates, Shibata Kyōhei and Satō Tetsuo. Mr. Shibata worked most closely with me during the course of the research project; his patient answers to many questions and

ACKNOWLEDGMENTS

critique of the final manuscript were essential to whatever insights I have obtained regarding Japanese agricultural development policy. Other professors deserving recognition are: Tanabe Hiroshi, Takahashi Akira, Kobori Iwao, Shimura Hiroyasu, Takahashi Yutaka, Senga Yūtarō, Okamoto Masami, Shirai Yoshihiko, Yuihama Shōgo, and Moritaki Kenichirō. In Saitama prefecture I received excellent cooperation from Yamamoto Shigeo, agricultural section chief, and Wada Hiroshi, administrative section chief, Minuma Land Improvement District Office.

Financial assistance in Japan came from a number of different sources, including the Rotary Foundation International (1980), the Inter-University Center for Japanese Language Studies (1980-81), the Japanese Ministry of Education (1980-82), the Japan Foundation (1983-84), and the Toyota Foundation (1980, 1982, and 1984, grants 80-1-192, 82-S-007, and 84-S-001, respectively). The staff of the Inter-University Center deserve special recognition for their excellent intensive and tutorial programs, which contributed immensely to my social and intellectual experiences in Japan. The Toyota Foundation graciously supported my work by assisting acquisition of research materials and by helping to overcome the high costs of transportation in the field; the opportunity to travel widely in the country was of incalculable benefit to my understanding of rural Japan.

My extended American and Japanese families have each provided pivotal support. My parents and sister, knowing they were partially responsible for instilling in me a curiosity about thought and culture, endured my long period of research in Japan without complaint. The Iwamura family, my surrogate home in Japan, extended to me all the warm encouragement anyone could hope to receive. Words can hardly describe the extraordinary support I have received from my wife, Elizabeth, and son, Noah. As fellow travelers on the road to and from Japan they, more than anyone, helped to sustain me in my work.

Finally, I wish to acknowledge the congeniality of my colleagues in geography at Portland State University. Their support, initially through a reduced teaching load and later through the PSU Cartographic Center, helped bring the research to completion. The onerous task of making the monograph "machine readable" was handled expertly by Carolyn L. Perry, to whom special appreciation is extended. Ichikawa Keiko, Portland State University; Miyamoto Mika, Aoyima Gakuin University; and Seth A. Reames, Sarjam Communications, were instrumental in the completion of the Japanese glossary. The illustrator for figures 1, 2, and 3 was Kuratomi Keiko.

All Japanese names in this publication follow the Japanese custom of writing the family name first.

INTRODUCTION

In recent years an increasing amount of research in English has begun to examine the agricultural development process in Japan. Such analysis, often oriented toward the historical evolution of the primary sector, typically measures increases in yield and labor productivity in terms of mechanization, scientific research on hybrid seeds and fertilizers, and commodity pricing policies.[1] Despite the broad scope of the literature, however, the formulation and implementation of post-World War II Japanese infrastructure investment policy have yet to be subjected to rigorous analysis. Such government-directed investment programs, commonly referred to as *tochi kairyō seisaku*, land improvement policy, attempt to upgrade the agricultural infrastructure in a variety of ways: through the establishment or refurbishing of irrigation and drainage networks; consolidation or reorganization of farmland; and expansion of the transportation system.

---

[1] Several representative examples of this approach are: Penelope Francks, *Technology and Agricultural Development in Pre-War Japan* (New Haven, Conn.: Yale University Press, 1983); Yūjirō Hayami, *A Century of Agricultural Growth in Japan* (Tokyo: University of Tokyo Press, 1975); Shigeru Ishikawa, *Economic Development in Asian Perspective* (Tokyo: Kinokuniya Bookstore Co., 1967); Takekazu Ogura, ed., *Agricultural Development in Modern Japan* (Tokyo: Fuji Publishing Co., 1967); Keizō Tsuchiya, *Productivity and Technological Progress in Japanese Agriculture* (Tokyo: Tokyo University Press, 1976); and Mitsuru Shimpo, *Three Decades in Shiwa: Economic Development and Social Change in a Japanese Farming Community* (Vancouver: University of British Columbia Press, 1976). A well-reasoned comment on the relationship between past and present conditions in Japan's primary sector is: John B. Cornell, review of *Technology and Agricultural Development in Pre-War Japan*, by Penelope Francks, *Journal of Asian History* 20, no. 1 (1986): 111-13. A recent and thorough review of the Japanese irrigation literature is William W. Kelly, *Irrigation Management in Japan: A Critical Review of Japanese Social Science Research* (Ithaca, N.Y.: Cornell University East Asia Papers, no. 30, 1982). A voluminous work identifying the many contemporary problems in the primary sector is Takekazu Ogura, *Can Japanese Agriculture Survive?* (Tokyo: Agricultural Policy Research Center, 1980). An additional representative work to be included here, but one not available for review at the time of publication, is Richard H. Moore, *Japanese Agriculture: Patterns of Rural Development* (Boulder: Westview, in press).

The analysis to follow focuses narrowly on an assessment of the role of land improvement policy in Japanese agricultural development, particularly in relation to the mainstay of the farming economy, wet-paddy[2] (rice) production.[3]

The general proposition guiding this research is that a major objective of post-World War II Japanese agricultural policy has been to articulate a comprehensive approach for rationalizing the use of land and water at the site of crop production.[4] The assumption that policy can promote coordinated decisions regarding land and water resource allocation in the agricultural sector deserves careful scrutiny. From a geographical perspective, it will be argued, the success or failure of such national policy depends on how effectively it identifies and overcomes those site-level obstacles which can interfere with program implementation. This point is to be examined through identification of: infrastructure investment characteristics in Japan; impediments to infrastructure development, both physical and cultural; and, most important, the degree to which coordinated development is promoted and accomplished by government policy. Land improvement policy concepts and projects will be analyzed in terms of national and prefectural data.

The methodology for analyzing infrastructure investment programs in post-World War II Japan calls for review of five main themes. Chapter 1 introduces and defines the descriptive terminology common to Japanese

---

[2] A common error in English (and Japanese literature in translation) is incorrect use of the appellation "paddy"; properly speaking, the term should refer to generic plant type, i.e., wet- or dry-paddy strains, and, further, it is not to be defined as a synonym for "field." The meaning of paddy is "rice," and linguistically it is Malay in origin (*padi*). Given this fact it is clearly redundant to refer to a wet-paddy field as a "rice paddy." The term "rice," where it does appear in this essay, will refer to the harvested wet-paddy crop.

[3] This is not to say that wet-paddy production is to be used synonymously with agricultural production, but that wet-paddy is to be recognized as the dominant field crop in Japan, both historically and in the present. (This point will be discussed further in chapter 2.) A good summary discussion of wet-paddy as a characteristic of Japanese agriculture can be found in: Francks, *Pre-War Agricultural Development*: 28-31; and Kelly, *Irrigation Management in Japan*: 1-3. A more comprehensive review of the characteristics of Japanese agriculture is Norton Ginsburg, "Economic and Cultural Geography," in *An Introduction to Japanese Civilization*, ed. Arthur E. Tiedemann (New York: Columbia University Press, 1974): 433-43.

[4] Gil Latz, *Nihon ni okeru kangai ni kan suru waei yōgo shū fuzuhyō* [Contemporary and Historical Irrigation in Japan--Selected Terminology and Illustrations] (Tokyo: Toyota Foundation, 1986): 5.

agricultural literature and policy.[5] Primary sector conditions, environmental and socioeconomic, are surveyed in chapter 2, focusing on the main features of wet-paddy agriculture in Japan. Chapter 3 discusses the policies promulgated by the Japanese government for land improvement; here attention is directed at the administrative and institutional framework for subsidizing infrastructure development, i.e., the Land Improvement District.[6] Following discussion of the wet-paddy cultivation cycle and government programs related to it, chapter 4 reports the findings of case-study analysis of Saitama prefecture in the Kantō plain immediately north of Tokyo. Emphasis is placed on the distribution of selected types of land improvement projects found there, particularly the administrative organizations responsible for agricultural investments in an important irrigation network, the Minumadai irrigation canal.[7] Chapter 5 concludes by evaluating the meaning and significance of the investment patterns identified. A key finding is that even though land improvement programs attempt to promote coordinated development of the agricultural infrastructure, land and especially water allocation decisions continue to be heavily influenced by traditional farming practices and customs in present-day Japan.

---

[5] A detailed discussion of Japanese agricultural terminology can be found in Latz, *Nihon ni okeru kangai* [Irrigation in Japan]. The reader may consult the appendix for an abbreviated glossary. Key Japanese terms are also listed in the index.

[6] See Latz, *Nihon ni okeru kangai* [Irrigation in Japan]: 36-41.

[7] A revised version of chapter 4 is Gil Latz, "Agricultural Infrastructure Development in Japan: The Case of Saitama Prefecture and the Minuma Land Improvement District," in *Proceedings: Research Exchange Symposium between Hokkaidō University and Portland State University, July 10-12, 1986*, ed. Executive Committee for Research Exchange Symposium between Hokkaidō University and Portland State University (Sapporo, Japan: Hokkaidō University, 1987): 1-66.

Chapter 1

THE LANGUAGE OF JAPANESE AGRICULTURE

The origins of this chapter can be traced to a recently completed analysis of the terminology used in the academic and governmental literature on Japanese irrigation practices.[1] Perhaps the key finding of this compilation can be stated as a simple linguistic imperative, namely, the importance of defining terminology when dealing with foreign language materials.[2] Although this is a prerequisite of all foreign area research, indeed all academic research, it takes on special meaning in the Japanese case because the basic geographical, social, and cultural characteristics of this country are quite different from those found in the West, particularly the United States. This point can be clarified further by looking in more detail at selected examples of the terminology used to describe the characteristics and policies of Japanese agriculture, followed by comment on the significance of such linguistic analysis to the methodology and objectives of this research project.

---

[1] Latz, *Nihon ni okeru kangai* [Irrigation in Japan]. A previous though partial summary of this work is: Nishikawa Osamu and Gil Latz, "The Role of Land Improvement Districts (*Tochi Kairyō Ku*) in the Modernization of Japan's Agricultural Sector: A Preliminary Research Report," *Proceedings*, Department of Humanities, College of General Education, University of Tokyo, 73 [*Tokyo Daigaku Kyōyōgaku-bu, Jinbunkagaku-ka Kiyō 73 (Jinbunchirigaku VII)*], Series on Human Geography no. 7 (March 1981): 53-70.

[2] Additional commentary regarding this observation about the Japanese terminology can be found in Latz, *Nihon ni okeru kangai* [Irrigation in Japan]: 1-3. (In chapter 1 the use of transliterated Japanese, when explaining the features of land improvement policy, is limited primarily to the footnotes. In subsequent chapters this format will change to one that includes, whenever possible, both Japanese and English appellations in the main text.)

The study of Japanese agriculture cannot proceed very far before the researcher confronts a number of examples of terminology with quite specialized usages. To begin with, according to 1982 statistics, 87 percent of all agriculturalists are classified as part-time farmers,[3] and of this group approximately 80 percent earn more than one-half of their income from nonagricultural employment.[4] This is an arresting statistic, suggesting as it must a set of social and economic circumstances quite at odds with the typical definition of "farmer."[5] Nor is this the only observation that calls attention to the need for careful scrutiny of the language used to describe the primary sector. Agricultural production in Japan has been dominated throughout history by small-scale cultivation of wet-paddy, a crop that is primarily dependent on controlled applications of water and capable of high yields almost regardless of soil fertility. The distinction between wet- and dry-field cultivation therefore becomes quite important, particularly the recognition of irrigation as a key feature of Japanese agriculture.[6]

---

[3]   In Japanese government documents, for example, the annual census, the term "farmer" is *sengyō nōka*, full-time farm household, that is, a farm household whose income is obtained exclusively from agricultural activity. In those cases where agricultural income is supplemented by other employment, the term *kengyō nōka*, part-time farm household, is used. There are two separate categories of *kengyō nōka*: (1) part-time farm households in which the major source of income is from agricultural activity (*dai isshu kengyō nōka*); and (2) part-time farm households in which reliance on agricultural income is supplemental (*dai nishu kengyō nōka*). See chart 1 for the declining number of full-time Japanese farmers.

[4]   Nōrinsuisanshō Keizaikyoku Tōkeijōhōbu, ed., *Poketto nōrin suisan tōkei 1983* [Agriculture, Forestry and Fisheries Statistics, 1983 Pocket Edition (Annual)] (Tokyo: Norin Tōkei Kyōkai, 1983): 123. In 1982, 70 percent of *all* Japanese farmers earned more than one-half of their income from nonagricultural employment.

[5]   This has led at least one geographer, David Kornhauser, to question the utility of the "farmer" designation when describing Japan's agricultural sector. This concern is implicit in Kornhauser's book, *Japan: Geographical Background to Urban-Industrial Development*, 2d ed. (London: Longman Group, 1982), especially chapter 2, pp. 34-57. In addition, Kornhauser has stated this view publicly at the 1985 Annual Meeting of the Association of American Geographers (at the conclusion to his presentation, "An Index of Urban Intensity for Japanese Cities, 1960-80").

[6]   The distinction between *suiden*, wet-paddy field, and *hatake*, dry-field, has long been recognized as a significant landscape feature of Japan. The complexity and function of irrigation networks loom large in any attempt to analyze this pattern of land use, a research theme of considerable interest to geographers and other social scientists. Representative examples are: Glenn T. Trewartha, *Japan: A Geography* (Madison: University of Wisconsin Press, 1965): 180-252; John D. Eyre, "Water Controls in a Japanese Irrigation System," *Geographical Review* 45, no. 2 (April 1955): 197-216; Ginsburg, "Economic and Cultural Geography," in *Introduction to Japanese Civilization*: 433-43; William W. Kelly, *Water Control in Tokugawa Japan: Irrigation Organization in a Japanese River Basin, 1600-1870* (Ithaca, N.Y.: Cornell University East Asia Papers no. 31, 1982): 1-14; Francks, *Pre-War Agricultural Development*: 28-35. More extensive definitions for these terms include: *suiden*, wet-paddy field--arable land that is dependent on irrigation networks to provide

If farmers in Japan, the crops they cultivate, and the methods of production do not fit standard Western definitions of agricultural activity, it follows that infrastructure development programs shaping the agricultural sector will also be characterized by specialized terminology usage. Investigation of this point leads to what might be referred to as the "administrative terminology" of Japanese agriculture, a hybrid collection of colloquial, civil engineering, and bureaucratic designations.[7] It is beyond the scope of this monograph to consider each element of this triad in a balanced fashion. Analysis will concentrate instead on those examples of language rooted in Japanese legislation for agricultural development, which will in turn allow us to isolate for the purposes of extended discussion specific government programs for creating a supporting infrastructure for wet-paddy production.

A review of the academic and governmental literature on Japanese agricultural policy[8] indicates that the term that most closely corresponds to

---

supplemental supplies of water in order to create a saturated medium for the growing of wet-paddy. Increasingly, such farmland may also have underdrainage facilities. A related term is *suiden nōgyō*, wet-paddy agriculture or wet-field agriculture. *Hatake*, dry field--arable land other than that used for wet-paddy or wet-field agriculture. Examples include vegetable growing areas, orchards, and meadows. See Latz, *Nihon ni okeru kangai* [Irrigation in Japan]: 43. According to Kelly, *kangai*, irrigation, is defined as "the entire cycle of agricultural water use . . . to include four phases: water source control, water delivery and distribution, in-field use, and drainage. Within each phase there are potentially four different types of tasks: construction of facilities, their maintenance and operation, water allocation, and conflict resolution." See Kelly, *Irrigation Management in Japan*: v-vi.

[7] Noted elsewhere is the disconcerting amount of ambiguity in the definitions of terms used to describe the contemporary agricultural production system; see Latz, *Nihon ni okeru kangai* [Irrigation in Japan]: 3-5; pp. 3-4 and 33-42 contain detailed commentary on jargon peculiar to academic and governmental literature on agricultural policy. An example of ambiguous usage of terminology is *seki*, weir, which can refer inclusively to dams, headworks, canals, or the entire irrigation network. Such confusion may be explained as an example of the different ways in which farmers and civil engineers describe irrigation and drainage facilities. In the farmer's case, the term for irrigation network may refer generally (in colloquial usage) to the entire network of canals, or a specific irrigation canal, based on local historical evolution of irrigation appellations. In contrast, contemporary engineering terminology uses the same designation to refer to specific structures within the irrigation network, e.g., dams, weirs, and headworks. Also, *tōshukō*, headworks, is a literal rendering in Japanese of the English term; this designation has not been used historically in Japan. For separate discussion of Japanese agricultural policies, see Moore, *Japanese Agriculture*, appendix A.

[8] The literature under review can be divided into two types: academic and governmental or government-related. In addition, a third major source of information was data collected in the field through interviews with government officials, farmers, and scholars, and in classes audited at the University of Tokyo between 1980 and 1983. Academic sources: Nishikawa Osamu, "Nihon ni okeru tochi riyō to tochi kairyō ni arawareta chiikiteki tokushoku" [Regional Characteristics of Land Use and Land Improvement in Japan], *Tokyo Daigaku Kyōyōgaku-bu, Jinbunkagaku-ka Kiyō (Jinbunchiri-gaku)* 34 (1965): 42-61; Nishikawa Osamu, "Nihon ni okeru tochi kairyō ku no bumpu" [The Distribution of Land Improvement Districts in Japan], *Tokyo Daigaku Kyōyōgaku-bu, Jinbunkagaku-ka Kiyō (Jinbunchiri-gaku)*

infrastructure development can be translated as "land improvement," *tochi kairyō*.[9] A number of observations about the literal meaning of this term are possible: it is not limited to arable land, nor does it contain overt reference to irrigation. But perhaps the most important observation is that

---

38 (1966): 17-24; Shirai Yoshihiko, *Nihon no kōchi seibi* [Land Improvement in Japan] (Tokyo: Taimeidō, 1972); Tamaki Akira, Hatate Isao, and Imamura Naraomi, *Suiri no shakai kōzō* [The Social Structure of Water Use] (Tokyo: Tokyo Daigaku Shuppan Kai, 1984); Shibata Kyōhei, "Daitoshi kinkō ni okeru nōgyō suiri soshiki no henyō--Saitama ken minuma tochi kairyō ku no baii " [Evolution and Response of Agricultural Water-Use Organizations to Suburbanization and Demand for Water Rationalization--The Case of the Minuma Land Improvement District], *Chigaku Zasshi* 94, no. 1 (1985): 1-20; Shibata Kyōhei, "Saitama ken minumadai yōsui ni okeru nōgyō suiri shisutemu--toshika e no taiō o chūshin ni" [Agricultural Water Use in Minumadai Canal of Saitama Prefecture--Centering on the Impact of Urbanization] (MS, March 1984); Shibata Kyōhei, "Nōgyō suiri no shisutemu ni kan suru ichikōsatsu--hōseijō no soshiki o chūshin ni" [One Consideration Concerning the Agricultural Water-Use System--Centered on the Organization of the Legal System], *Tokyo Daigaku Kyōyōgaku-bu, Jinbunkagaku-ka, Kiyō 78 (Jinbunchiri-gaku 8)* 78 (March 1983): 65-89; Imamura Naraomi et al., *Tochi kairyō hyaku nen shi* [A Hundred Years of Land Improvement] (Tokyo: Heibonsha, 1977); Yamazaki Fujio, *Nōchi kōgaku* [Agricultural Land Civil Engineering] (Tokyo: Tokyo Daigaku Shuppan Kai, 1977); Kaneko Ryō, ed., *Nōgyō suimon gaku* [Agricultural Hydrology] (Tokyo: Kyōritsu Publishing Co., 1978); Isozaki Hisashi, ed., *Kangai haisui* [Irrigation and Drainage] (Tokyo: Yōkendō Co., 1978); Ishibashi Yutaka et al., *Nōgyō suiri gaku* [Agricultural Water Use] (Tokyo: Asakura Shoten, 1977).

Governmental or government-related literature: Okabe Saburō, *Zusetsu tochi kairyō 100 kō--asu no nōson kensetsu o mezashite* [One Hundred Lectures on Land Improvement--Toward Future Rural Development] (Tokyo: Chikusha, 1979); Nōrinsuisanshō Kōzōkaizenkyoku Kensetsubu, ed., *Tochi kairyō no zenyō--kaisetsu to shiryō* [Comprehensive Summary of Land Improvement--Explanation and Data] (Tokyo: Kōkyōjigyō Tsūshinsha, 1982); Nōgyō Suiri Kenkyūkai, ed., *Nihon no nōgyō yōsui* [Agricultural Water Use in Japan] (Tokyo: Chikusha, 1980); Nōrinsuisanshō Kōzōkaizenkyoku, ed., *Tochi kairyō hō kaisetsu* [Land Improvement Law Commentary] (Tokyo: Zenkoku Tochi Kairyō Jigyō Dantai Rengō Kai, 1974 (rev. ed.); Nōrinsuisanshō Kōzōkaizenkyoku, *Tochi kairyō jigyō keikaku sekkei kijun--hojō seibi (suiden)* [Standard Design Plans for Land Improvement Projects--Farmland Consolidation (Wet-Paddy Field)] (Tokyo: Nōrinsuisanshō Kōzōkaizenkyoku, 1977). See also six other volumes published by this government agency between 1977 and 1981 concerning plan designs for: *hojō seibi (hatake)* [Farmland Consolidation (Dry Field)]; *nōchi kaihatsu (kaibatake)* [Farmland Development (Dry Field)]; *haisui* [Drainage]; *ankyo haisui* [Field Under-drainage]; *nōchi hozen* [Agricultural Land Protection]; and *nōdō* [Agricultural Roads]; and Japanese Society of Irrigation, Drainage, and Reclamation Engineering, International Affairs Commission, ed., *Irrigation and Drainage in Japan Pictorial* (Tokyo: Japanese Society of Irrigation, Drainage, and Reclamation Engineering, 1978).

9   The term *tochi kairyō*, land improvement, has yet to be subjected to rigorous, extended analysis in the English literature. Perhaps one of the reasons for this is the general confusion surrounding the meaning and usage of this designation in the Japanese literature. This point is considered in some detail by Shirai Yoshihiko, *Nihon no kōchi seibi*. In the introduction to his analysis, Shirai distinguishes clearly between land improvement as an object of government policy and the specific infrastructure investment projects for realizing this goal. Thus he eschews the term *tochi kairyō* and replaces it with *kōchi seibi*. The literal translation of the latter is "farmland consolidation," which concentrates especially on arable land exchange and consolidation and field shape alteration (replotment).

this appellation does not concern development in the conventional sense of creating something new; instead, the emphasis is on the improvement of what already exists. Figure 1 presents one example of such agricultural development, a comprehensive revamping of the traditional field layout for the purpose of improving water control and elevating the degree of mechanization.[10] The reader might note here a host of features which distinguish agricultural production in Japan, including the small scale of landholdings, the importance of access to water, water control, relatively undeveloped uplands, and the agglomerated village settlement form.

Policy programs for land improvement, or land improvement projects, can be traced back to the turn of the century and are distinguished by their extraordinary variety.[11] Included under the purview of this policy are projects for the development of the arable land infrastructure ranging from farmland consolidation to soil dressing; the upgrading of the water distribution network, including dam construction, irrigation canal refurbishing, or construction of drainage facilities; land reclamation; natural disaster prevention in the form of protective dikes or levees; the upgrading of the transportation network; and village infrastructure development, e.g., park (recreational) facilities. The range of activities is remarkably broad, but it should be pointed out that the policy did not appear in the full form noted above, but evolved over time to its present complexity. Thus, although an early objective was farmland replotment (1899), such reorganization proved to be less popular than irrigation and drainage projects (1909, 1923). In the post-World War II period, land improvement programs included even village infrastructure investments in the form of park facilities (1972-73). All of these projects are land improvements, but at the same time, they represent a pattern of infrastructure development characterized by changing

---

[10] Figure 1 is adapted from Nōrinsuisanshō, *Tochi kairyō no zenyō* [Comprehensive Summary of Land Improvement], 1982: i, 31. An additional fourteen illustrations pertaining to Japan's irrigated agricultural areas can be found in Latz, *Nihon ni okeru kangai* [Irrigation in Japan]: 65-79. See also figures 2 and 3.

[11] Japanese government policy for land improvement originated in the late nineteenth century with the enactment of the *Kōchi Seiri Hō*, Arable Land Reorganization Law (no. 82), in 1899 (Meiji 32). Full articulation of land improvement as a policy concept, however, occurs in the *Tochi Kairyō Hō*, Land Improvement Law (no. 195), in 1949 (Showa 24). The land improvement appellation is both general, in that it refers to all projects authorized by the 1949 legislation, and specific, in that it refers to certain facilities necessary for physical infrastructure development at a local agricultural site. Precisely speaking, land improvement projects, *tochi kairyō jigyō*, aim at amelioration of site conditions inhibiting agricultural production; administratively there were about eighty different types as of 1984. See: Latz, *Nihon ni okeru kangai* [Irrigation in Japan]: 37; and chapter 3, below.

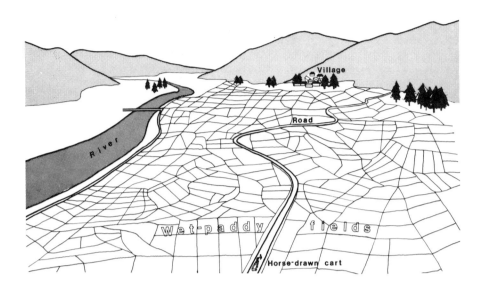

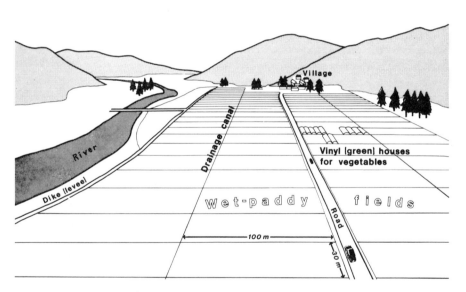

Fig. 1. The process of farmland consolidation in Japan.
Adapted from Nōrinsuisanshō, *Tochi kairyō no zenyō* [Comprehensive Summary of Land Improvement], 1982: i, 31. Site: Akita prefecture. Illustrator: Kuratomi Keiko.

goals for farm communities in Japan.[12]

Although there has been considerable evolution in the policy of and projects for land improvement, the site-level administrative structure acting as a conduit for infrastructure investment, referred to variously as Arable Land Reorganization Associations or Land Improvement Districts, has remained a relatively constant feature of Japanese agricultural development policy.[13] These administrative organizations are charged, by law, with responsibility for collecting assessed fees from those farmers benefiting from

---

[12]   This brief sentence pinpoints a central problem with broad generalizations about the meaning of *tochi kairyō*, land improvement, that is, failure to consider and account for the changing objectives of the corresponding agricultural policies. It is quite common, for example, for the term "land improvement" to refer to all investments related to the arable land infrastructure, including construction of water control facilities, for the period 1899 to the present. However, this generalization ignores differences between the pre- and post-World War II policies for land improvement, that is, between the *Kōchi Seiri Hō*, Arable Land Reorganization Law of 1899, and the *Tochi Kairyō Hō*, Land Improvement Law of 1949. Not only are there specific differences between each piece of legislation, but revisions subsequent to enactment also must be taken into account. Thus, in the original legislation of 1899 the goal was farmland replotment, but by means of the revision of 1909 greater emphasis was placed on irrigation and drainage projects. The irrigation and drainage theme continues to the present, including enactment of separate guidelines in 1923, Rules for Subsidization of Irrigation and Drainage Projects, *Yōhaisui Kairyō Jigyō Hojo Yōkō*, as well as the Land Improvement Law of 1949. In the most recent legislation, however, there has been a notable increase in land improvement projects which aim at dry-field development, transportation system expansion, and village infrastructure rationalization. All of these points underscore the need for precise terminology definition when describing the objectives of land improvement policies.

[13]   The name and function for each organization differ according to date of promulgation. The *Kōchi Seiri Kumiai*, Arable Land Reorganization Association, was initiated in 1909 (disbanded in 1952), as part of the revisions in that year for the *Kōchi Seiri Hō*, Arable Land Reorganization Law of 1899. This organization served as the administrative vehicle for carrying out projects for land exchange and consolidation, field shape alteration, reclamation, conversion of dry-field to wet-paddy agriculture, and construction of irrigation and drainage facilities. A related organization, but one operating without government subsidy, was the *Futsū Suiri Kumiai*, Regular Water-Use Association, initiated in 1890 (disbanded in 1952); its function was to collect monies for irrigation network maintenance. The origin of this organization can be traced to the 1890 Ordinance for Water-Use Associations, *Suiri Kumiai Jōrei*, although its twentieth-century legal status was established through revisions in 1908 to the Regular Water-Use Association Law. In both of the above mentioned cooperative organizations, membership was confined to landlords; this requirement was liberalized according to the Land Improvement Law of 1949 when a new administrative organization was created, the Land Improvement District, *Tochi Kairyō Ku*. While the district's organizational features can be linked to these earlier entities, it is not necessarily concerned exclusively with farmland consolidation and water-use activities, but is involved also in a variety of projects for rural development. By law the district is the site-level entity responsible for cost-sharing negotiations with higher levels of government. Maintenance costs for established facilities are borne generally by this local organization. The total number, as of March 31, 1981, was 9,147; this figure has declined slowly from a peak of 13,146 in 1961. See Latz, *Nihon ni okeru kangai* [Irrigation in Japan]: 33-34, 36-38.

a given land improvement project. This task is accomplished, in part, through use of limited coercive powers to force farmer participation. The advantages of participation are many, including access to inexpensive credit from government financial organs as well as the support of expert technicians and civil servants highly proficient at developing either technical or policy proposals designed to ameliorate those circumstances which interfere with agricultural production. Over the course of the twentieth century the number, scale, objectives, subsidy provisions, and rights of participation have all changed, but the organization itself has persisted, becoming one of the enduring features of Japanese agriculture.

The promulgation of policy for land improvement is directly related to the disappearance of the conventional agricultural frontier in the early twentieth century (with the exception of northeastern Japan and parts of Hokkaidō), which led to a program designed to promote more intensive land use in order to meet the increasing food consumption needs of the nation. Since 1920, in fact, there has been little increase in the gross amount of arable land in Japan, and the rise in yield is due, therefore, to the increasing sophistication and intensity of production techniques.[14] A small but growing body of work in English has examined this feature of Japanese agriculture, primarily from an economic point of view, noting that land scarcity has been one of the major limiting factors of agricultural production.[15] This research has also documented that by the early 1900s, infra-

---

[14] The relationship between the halt in the gross expansion of the cultivated area and policies prompting investment in the arable land infrastructure is discussed in Ishikawa, *Development in Asian Perspective*: 61-69; and Hayami, *Century of Agricultural Growth*: 174-79, 184-89, 195-99. A good discussion of the changing regional concentration of wet-paddy production in the twentieth century can be found in Akira Ebato, *Postwar Japanese Agriculture* (Tokyo: International Society for Educational Information Press, 1973): 17-21. The identification of high-yielding varieties of wet-paddy, the basis of continued increases in total volume of harvested rice, can be found in Francks, *Pre-War Agricultural Development*: 55-63, 76-85; and Hayami, *Century of Agricultural Growth*: 48-59. One thoughtful and concise statement of these characteristics of Japanese agriculture is Yoshikatsu Ogasawara's "The Role of Rice and Rice Paddy [sic] Development in Japan," *Bulletin of the Geographical Survey Institute* 5, pt. 4 (March 1958): 1-23.

[15] Representative examples include: Hayami, *Century of Agricultural Growth*; Francks, *Pre-War Agricultural Development*; Ishikawa, *Development in Asian Perspective*; Ogura, ed., *Agricultural Development*; Tsuchiya, *Progress in Japanese Agriculture*; K. Ohkawa, Bruce Johnston, and H. Kaneda, *Agriculture and Economic Growth--Japan's Experience* (Tokyo: University of Tokyo Press, 1969); James Nakamura, *Agricultural Production and the Economic Development of Japan 1873 to 1922* (Princeton, N.J.: Princeton University Press, 1966); Ronald P. Dore, "Agricultural Improvement in Japan," *Economic Development and Cultural Change* 9, no. 1, pt. 2 (October 1960): 69-91.; M. Akino, "Land Infrastructure Improvement in Agricultural Development: The Japanese Case, 1900 to 1965," *Economic Development and Cultural Change* 28, no. 1 (October 1979): 97-117; Japan Economic Research Center, ed., *Agriculture and Economic Development--Structural Readjustment in Asian Perspective*, 2 vols. (Tokyo: Japan Economic Research Center, 1972); William Lockwood, *The State and Economic Enterprise in*

structure investment, as well as scientific research on hybrid seeds and fertilizers, led to a higher economic return than did continued expansion of the arable land base. Such agricultural development programs have depended heavily on subsidization from the public sector, owing, in part, to the need to sustain a growing population and provide urban laborers in the burgeoning industrial sector with low-cost supplies of food, and in part to the relative scarcity of capital on the part of most landowners.

Projects for infrastructure investment are significant because they represent a fundamental shift in twentieth-century Japanese agricultural development policy. The basis of this observation may be found in the three key factors referred to above: (1) disappearance of the conventional agricultural frontier; (2) formulation of new research programs for increasing yield, based on the identification of both hybrid seeds and suitable fertilizers; and (3) an emphasis on such infrastructure investment as farmland replotment and the renovation or establishment of irrigation and drainage networks. It should be underscored, furthermore, that this transformation of agricultural development policy is symbolized conceptually by the changing language of Japanese agriculture, particularly the emergence since the turn of the century of administrative terminology (e.g., "land improvement").

A note of caution: it is probably incorrect to see land improvement as a completely new phenomenon in Japan's primary sector. A more accurate description would identify the relationship between land improvement and two long-standing concerns of the Japanese farmer, the need to create farmland by means of land reclamation,[16] and recognition of the crucial importance of irrigation to successful crop production. It is intriguing to note in the case of land reclamation that its meaning, often defined in the literature as a process of "land ripening," or the "bringing of a site to a state of

---

Japan (Princeton, N.J.: Princeton University Press, 1968); E. Crawcour, "Japan 1869-1920," in *Agricultural Development in Asia*, ed. R. Shand (Canberra: Australian National University Press, 1969): 1-24.

[16] The term "land reclamation" has an extremely broad meaning, as reflected by the fact that three designations are commonly used in Japanese: *kaikon, nōchi zōsei, kaitaku.* Each term refers generally to the development of agricultural land, including wet-paddy fields, dry fields, orchards, and pastureland, through conversion of uncultivated woodlands and plains. There is also specific reference, in the case of *nōchi zōsei*, to reclamation in extremely wet areas, by means of landfill or land draining, e.g., Hachirōgata, Akita prefecture. General rural development objectives may also be included in the case of *kaitaku*, e.g., the emergency land reclamation projects, *kinkyū kaitaku jigyō*, which aimed at expanding the amount of arable land in Japan immediately after World War II. See Latz, *Nihon ni okeru kangai* [Irrigation in Japan]: 48.

optimum production (fruition),"[17] is remarkably similar to the objectives of contemporary land improvement projects for the agricultural infra-structure. Furthermore, as is well documented in both the Japanese and English literature on the history of agricultural development, Japan entered the modern period with a relatively sophisticated water distribution net-work already in place. According to one estimate, 72.3 percent of all irriga-tion facilities operating in the 1960s were established during the Tokugawa period, 1603-1867.[18] But whereas land improvement programs may be traced to the traditional practices of land reclamation or irrigation construc-tion, they have been promoted as national policy only since the turn of the century. Accompanying such recognition of the inherent potential of the existing arable land base was a degree of public attention, and an infusion of public monies into the agricultural sector,[19] that was unprecedented in Japanese history. In short, although the practice of land improvement may be seen as a modern version of traditional approaches to elevating agri-cultural yield in Japan, the policy for realizing this goal was distinctively new.

It is remarkable that the English literature on Japanese agriculture has paid only incidental attention to enactment of land improvement legisla-tion. It does not receive explicit consideration, for example, in any of the six main focuses of contemporary research, including: land reform; the agricul-tural cooperative system; price controls (subsidies) for the staple foodstuff, rice; the relationship between technology and agricultural development; investment in basic research facilities; or the problems with international trade.[20] As a result, perspective on the characteristics of the Japanese agri-

---

[17] See Latz, *Nihon ni okeru kangai* [Irrigation in Japan]: 5, 48. I would like to acknowledge Nishikawa Osamu, University of Tokyo, for explanation of this point.

[18] S. Sawada, "The Development of Rice Productivity in Japan: Pre-War Experience," in *Agriculture and Economic Development*, ed. Japan Economic Research Center (Tokyo: Japan Economic Research Center, 1972): 115-40. The 72.3 percent figure represents an average for both pond/reservoir facilities (70.9 percent) and river-based irrigation networks (73.7 per-cent). See also Francks, *Pre-War Agricultural Development:* 32.

[19] Hayami, *Century of Agricultural Growth:* 198-99.

[20] The only partial exception to this generalization about research in English is examin-ation of the relationship between policy, technology, and agricultural development. See: Hayami, *Century of Agricultural Growth:* 46-83 (note especially comment on pre-World War II institutional innovation, pp. 171-74); Ishikawa, *Development in Asian Perspective:* 96-109, 142-53; Tsuchiya, *Progress in Japanese Agriculture:* 201-23; Francks, *Pre-War Agricultural Development:* 25-46, 76-93; Kelly, *Irrigation Management in Japan:* 37-59; Ogura, ed., *Agricultural Development:* 232-95, 388-409; and Ogura, *Can Japanese Agriculture Survive?:* 198-264, 371-468. In each case, however, commentary on policies for land improvement in the post-World War II period is cursory, at best. In contrast, study of land improvement programs is a moderately well developed theme in the Japanese literature.

cultural sector is biased in several respects. At the most general level there is heavy emphasis on analysis of commodity production and marketing in the research themes identified above. Second, when policy is analyzed as part of the development process, the economic, technological, and biological aspects of the government programs are stressed, but little attention is directed to the administrative organizations through which government investment takes place, such as the aforementioned Land Improvement District. Third, in contrast to the approach found in this research project, little attention is directed to the administrative terminology spawned by these programs for agricultural development; nor is there sufficient speculation about the possible significance of such language. Finally, when analysis of infrastructure investment does take place there is a preoccupation with Japan's early twentieth-century experience, to the neglect of the post-

---

Two programs of the Allied occupation, the land reform and restructuring of the agricultural cooperative association, are credited with having a major impact on post-World War II agricultural development. The land reform, as is well known, created a class of independent yeoman farmers, in contrast to the prewar landlord/tenant system, and the restructuring of the cooperative association deemphasized political and ideological objectives while retaining a nationwide organizational structure capable of disseminating technical information and encouraging commodity marketing. Price controls for the staple foodstuff, rice, can also be mentioned. This policy dates to wartime decisions by the Japanese government, e.g., the Staple Foodstuff Control System, *Shokuryō Kanri Seido*. This program was reinforced during the Allied Occupation and has since been manipulated by special interest groups to grant farmers a high guaranteed income from wet-paddy cultivation. A fourth example, government investment in research facilities, calls attention to funding for development of hybrid seeds and fertilizers well-suited to the environmental conditions in Japan. Finally, a conscious decision was made by Japanese policy makers to import certain commodities, particularly soybeans, soft white wheat, and fodder for cattle production.

Research in the English literature that discusses how these and other government policies have stimulated agricultural production includes: Ronald P. Dore, *Land Reform in Japan* (London: Oxford University Press, 1959); Tadashi Fukutake, *Rural Society in Japan* (Tokyo: Tokyo University Press, 1980): 184-209; Gen Itasaka, ed., *Encyclopedia of Japan* 1, s.v. "Agriculture" (Tokyo: Kōdansha Publishing Co., 1983); Michael W. Donnelly, "Setting the Price of Rice: A Study in Political Decision Making," in *Policy-Making in Contemporary Japan*, ed. T. J. Pempel (Ithaca, N.Y.: Cornell University Press, 1977): 143-200; Michael W. Donnelly, "The Future of Japanese Agriculture" (review article) *Pacific Affairs* 53, no. 4 (Winter 1980-81): 708-16; Aurelia D. George, "The Japanese Farm Lobby and Agricultural Policy-Making," *Pacific Affairs* 54, no. 3 (Fall 1981): 409-30; William T. Coyle, *Japan's Rice Policy* (Washington, D.C.: United States Department of Agriculture, Economic and Statistics Service, Foreign Agricultural Economic Report no. 164, 1981); Fred H. Sanderson, *Japan's Food Prospects and Policies* (Washington, D.C.: Brookings Institution, 1978): 5-16; Albert Ravenholt, "The Japanese Farmer: Wheat or Rice for the Yen?" *American Universities Field Staff Reports*, Asia, 1978, no. 18; Kenzō Hemmi, "Agriculture and Politics in Japan," in *U.S.-Japanese Agricultural Trade Relations*, ed. Emery Castle and Kenzō Hemmi (Baltimore: Johns Hopkins University Press, 1982): 219-72; and Saburō Okita, "The Proper Approach to Food Policy," *Japan Echo* 5, no. 2 (Summer 1978): 49-57.

World War II effects of industrialization and urbanization on the primary sector.[21]

The chapters that follow will provide more detailed examination of the contemporary Japanese policy for land improvement. The investigation will concentrate on the characteristics of this policy in the post-World War II period, particularly the legal framework created to channel investment into the infrastructure supporting crop production in irrigated agricultural areas.[22] The overall aim is to identify the meaning, objectives, accomplishments, and future prospect of this policy. My approach will concentrate on careful definition of the administrative terminology related to the policy for land improvement, a perspective grounded in the preceding review of selected examples of the relationship between the language of Japanese agriculture and twentieth-century policy for infrastructure investment.

---

[21] This is a key point, for the problem is not that research in English on Japanese agricultural policy is lacking, but that little of it looks at policy in the context of post-World War II urbanization and industrialization influences. See Gil Latz, "The Persistence of Agricultural Activity in Urban Japan: An Analysis of the Tokyo Metropolitan Area," in *The Extended Metropolis in Asia*, ed. Norton Ginsburg and T. G. McGee (Honolulu: University of Hawaii Press, in press). This problem is slowly being addressed, either in terms of the "crises" facing Japanese agriculture or through analysis of agriculture and high technology. Three cases in point are: the comments by Michael W. Donnelly in "The Future of Japanese Agriculture"; and, more recently, the session organized by John B. Cornell at the 1985 Association of Asian Studies Meetings, "Japanese Agriculture: The Crisis of Family Farming and Structural Reform"; as well as the session organized by Susan O. Long at the 1987 Association of Asian Studies Meetings, "High Tech and 'High Touch': The Meanings of Technology in Japanese Agriculture and Fishing." In terms of the proposed research, however, it would seem comments in a recent book review of two works by William Kelly (*Irrigation Management in Japan* and *Water Control in Tokugawa Japan*), are more pertinent: "As far as irrigation in Japanese agriculture today is concerned, there is some doubt in the reviewer's mind that the subject is now of vital interest . . . compared either to its central importance in the past or to current and future needs for water and water management in both the modern industrial and commercial sectors and for settlement and other non-commercial use. Mr. Kelly's writings are thus crucial to an understanding of . . . agrarian tradition, but they may relate less strongly to the circumstances of the present." David H. Kornhauser, review, *Monumentica Nipponica* 37, no. 4 (1985): 465-66. The accuracy of Kornhauser's observation is discussed further in chapters 4 and 5, below.

[22] See also Latz, *Nihon ni okeru kangai* [Irrigation in Japan]: 3-5.

Chapter 2

THE JAPANESE AGRICULTURAL LANDSCAPE

Chapter 1 analyzed briefly the language used in the Japanese agricultural literature, calling attention to the importance of terminology definition. The perspective in the paragraphs to follow will shift analysis to the environmental and socioeconomic characteristics of the primary sector with the distinctive features of the agricultural landscape serving as its basis.

The Distribution of Arable Land

The island country of Japan, arcuate in form and volcanic in origin, is located in the western Pacific Ocean adjacent to the Eurasian landmass between 20 and 46 degrees latitude north. (See map 1).[1] Totaling 377,728 square kilometers in land area, and composed of four main islands and thousands of smaller ones, the country is distinctively mountainous, narrow, and elongated, with a length from northeast to southwest exceeding 3,500 kilometers. Arable land comprises 14.5 percent of the total land area, slightly more than 5.4 million hectares, according to 1982 statistics.[2] Given

---

[1]   Japanese territory, including the disputed Kurile Islands of Kunashiri, Etorofu, Shikotan, and the Habomai group, can be delimited as latitude north: 45 degrees 33 minutes to 20 degrees 25 minutes; longitude east: 153 degrees 59 minutes to 122 degrees 56 minutes.

[2]   To clarify this point: the total arable land base during the post-World War II period remained relatively stable at about 6 million hectares until 1965; increasing competition with urban land uses, as well as diversion of marginal land in mountainous areas for timber production, reduced this figure to a 1982 total of 5,426,000 hectares. Basic references for statistical data on the contemporary Japanese agricultural sector can be found in the following sources: Itasaka, ed. *Encyclopedia of Japan* 1: 21-32; Nōrinsuisanshō Keizaikyoku Tōkeijōhōbu, ed. *Poketto nōrin suisan tōkei, 1983* [Agriculture, Forestry and Fisheries Statistics, 1983, Pocket Edition]: 107-304; Japan, Ministry of Agriculture, Forestry and Fisheries, Statistics and Information Department, ed., *Abstract of Statistics on Agriculture, Forestry and Fisheries: Japan/1982* (Tokyo: Association of Agriculture, Forestry and Fishery Statistics, 1983): 1-86; Kuroda, "The Present State of Agriculture in Japan," in *U.S.-Japanese*

current population levels, in excess of 120,000,000 people,[3] Japan may be characterized as having an unfavorable balance between population and arable land resources. Physiographic population density is high, approximately 2,200 people per square kilometer, and food self-sufficiency ratios are moderate, standing at 70 percent as of 1980.[4]

The most striking feature of the Japanese agricultural landscape is the distribution of arable land, and the extent to which it is devoted to wet-paddy cultivation. Statistics indicate that approximately 48 percent of the total cultivated area, 2.6 million hectares, is devoted to wet-paddy production. Dry-field agriculture makes up the balance, with orchard and pastureland each accounting for 11 percent, respectively.[5] Most of this agricultural land, including virtually all of the wet-paddy cultivation, is concentrated in the alluvial lowlands, in the diluvial uplands, and adjacent to or on top of the lakes and swamps that make up approximately one-quarter of the total land area. The remainder of the archipelago, composed of rugged uplands with steep slopes inclined by more than eight degrees, is covered by mixed deciduous and evergreen forests. In general terms Japan can be described as

---

Agricultural Trade Relations, ed. Castle and Hemmi: 91-147; Hayami, *Century of Agricultural Growth:* 170-92; Ebato, *Postwar Japanese Agriculture:* 17-44; Kenji Ishimitsu and Junko Gotō, "Changing Rural Areas as the Object of Rural Planning in Japan," *Journal of Irrigation Engineering and Rural Planning*, no. 2 (July 1982): 28-42; Fukutake, *Rural Society in Japan:* 1-26; Ogura, *Can Japanese Agriculture Survive?:* 673-798.

[3]   According to the Statistics Bureau, Management Coordination Agency, Japan's population was 120,017,647 as of July 1, 1984.

[4]   Physiographic population density (the ratio between population and arable land) and self-sufficiency ratios (the dependence on commodity importation to meet consumption needs) summarize the degree of population pressure on Japan's agricultural resources. In the case of the latter, the percentage varies according to terminology definition and research objective. The figure listed here is taken from *Nōrinsuisanshō, Nōgyō hakusho fuzoku tōkeihyō* (annual) [Agricultural White Paper on Statistical Matters] (Tokyo: Nōrinsuisanshō, 1981). This information is reproduced in English in Itasaka, ed., *Encyclopedia of Japan* 1: 31. (Japan's food self-sufficiency ratio increases to 77 percent if all foodstuffs, including fishery products, are included. However, it decreases considerably, to a level of 51 percent, if measured in terms of original food energy, as calculated by Sanderson, *Japan's Food Prospects and Policies:* 5-16.)

[5]   According to 1982 statistics, the total area under cultivation was 5.43 million hectares; 55.5 percent were classified as *suiden*, wet-paddy fields, and 44.5 percent *hatake*, dry fields. As of this date, however, wet-paddy was actually cultivated on only 48 percent of all arable land owing to crop diversification policies implemented in 1970. This statistical discrepancy derives from the fact that not all land capable of wet-paddy production is now being used for this purpose. Compare the following two sources: Japan, Ministry of Agriculture, *Abstracts of Agriculture Statistics, 1982:* 1-3; and James P. Houck, "Agreements and Policy in U.S.-Japanese Agricultural Trade," in *U.S.-Japanese Agricultural Trade Relations*, ed. Emery Castle and Kenzō Hemmi (Baltimore: Johns Hopkins University Press, 1982): 61-63.

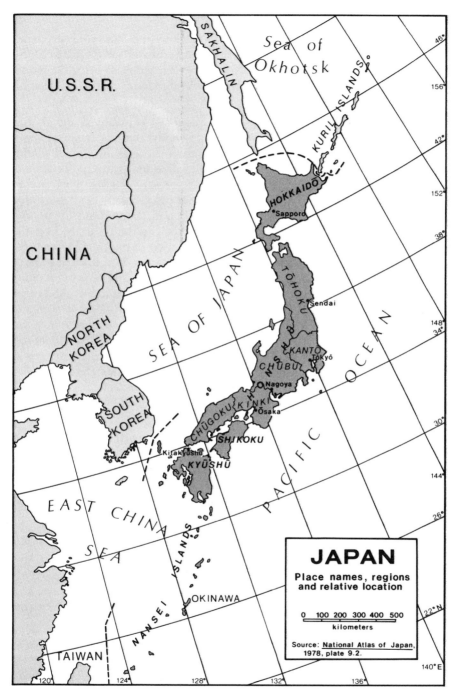

Map 1. *Japan: place names, regions, and relative location.*

a country of extensive forested uplands with low population density, and intensively used agricultural lowlands devoted primarily to wet-paddy cultivation, with high population density. The concentration of urban land-use activity found in these lowland areas, particularly along the Pacific coast of Japan, reinforces this fact of human geography.[6]

Environmental circumstances have played a key role in the evolution of the Japanese agricultural landscape. The fact that the Japanese have shown a marked preference over time to settle in and develop lowland areas is often attributed to the nature of the predominantly mountainous terrain, a by-product of the relatively recent volcanic origins of the archipelago.[7] In addition, two other environmental processes that influence the distribution of arable land are soil formation and the amount of annual precipitation. The soils of Japan, whether podzolic to the north, or lateritic to the south, are immature, with poorly developed horizons. Soil fertility, therefore, is generally mediocre, although it increases in the alluvial lowlands where agricultural activity is concentrated. In the case of precipitation, Japan is by and large water rich. In an average year, for example, total rainfall is approximately 1,800 millimeters, and the maximum amount of available water resources is equal to some 450 billion cubic meters.[8] A midlatitude location, in combination with the complex climatic interaction of the Pacific Ocean and Eurasian landmass, creates the modified monsoon effect that is largely responsible for this situation. One characteristic of the monsoon in Japan is the early summer rainy season, *baiu*, which affects all parts of the country except Hokkaidō, and acts as a major stimulus to wet-paddy production.

The dependence of wet-paddy on large amounts of water during the growing period reinforces the significance of the alluvial lowlands, by definition catchments for upland runoff. The advantage of utilizing land in these lowlands is that water can be more easily controlled for distribution purposes through reliance on gravity-fed irrigation canals.[9] The sources of

---

[6] This observation is well developed by Kornhauser, *Japan*: 3-7. See also Francks, *Agricultural Development in Pre-War Japan*: 49-55.

[7] A comprehensive discussion of the physical geography of Japan is in Torao Yoshikawa et al., *The Landforms of Japan* (Tokyo: University of Tokyo Press, 1981). (The significance many Japanese attach to the mountainous nature of the archipelago, as a determining influence on both national character and national settlement patterns, should be underscored.)

[8] This figure takes into consideration evapotranspiration loss; see Japan, Water Resources Bureau, National Land Agency, "Water Resources in Japan" (Tokyo: Water Resources Bureau, National Land Agency, 1977): 3.

[9] A more detailed discussion of the characteristics of Japanese irrigation networks will be found in chapter 3; see figures 2 and 3.

water for these irrigation networks can be either rivers or reservoirs, with the former accounting for some 70 percent of the irrigated area.[10] Farmers hold the bulk of all water-use rights in Japan, both by law and custom, and agricultural requirements alone accounted for 63 percent of water use in 1975.[11] The large amount of water represented by this percentage is due to a peculiar feature of wet-paddy production, the aquatic growing medium of this plant.[12] Therefore, timely distribution is crucial not only for maintaining field water depth and field flooding after the midsummer drainage period, but also for surface soil puddling prior to seedling transplanting in early spring.[13] Agricultural water demand is highest during the wet-paddy cultivation period from late March to late September.

---

[10] Francks, *Pre-War Japanese Agriculture*, 1983: 33. *Tameike*, pond/small reservoirs, account for 20 percent of the contemporary irrigated area, with miscellaneous other techniques affecting the remaining 10 percent.

[11] Total demand for water in 1975 equaled 90,000 million tons: 14 percent was for domestic purposes, 23 percent was for industrial purposes, and the remainder was for agricultural purposes. Japan, National Land Agency, "Water Resources Policy in Japan" (Tokyo: National Land Agency, National Land Policy Series no. 3, 1977): 3.

[12] The term "aquatic" requires special definition. As Grist has noted, "The supply and control of water . . . is the most important aspect of irrigated paddy cultivation; given an adequate and well-controlled water supply the crop will grow in a wide range of soils and in many climates. It is therefore more important than the type of soil." See D. H. Grist, *Rice* (London: Longman, 1959): 28, 29; and Clifford Geertz, *Agricultural Involution: The Process of Ecological Change in Indonesia* (Berkeley: University of California Press, 1963): 30. Geertz elaborates on the fundamental importance of water control as follows: "This primary reliance on the material which envelops the biotic community (the "medium") for nourishment rather than on the solid surface in which it is rooted (the "substratum"), makes possible the same maintenance of an effective agricultural regime on indifferent soils that the direct cycling pattern of energy exchange makes possible on swidden" (p. 30).

[13] Water management in wet-paddy fields relies on a complex set of irrigation procedures in order to maintain water depth requirements during the cultivation period. Irrigation begins with the introduction of water for surface soil puddling in the early spring. Water level is subsequently maintained in the fields until the midsummer drainage period in late July/early August, after which the fields are flooded once again. Residual water is drained in September in order to ensure that the field is thoroughly dry by harvest. These procedures may be unfamiliar to the reader, and are defined as follows. Irrigation, *kangai*, is a highly controlled process of conducting water systematically to arable lands, including its regional distribution under careful supervision for cultivation purposes, which thereby raises agricultural productivity. Such water transfer is highly dependent on sophisticated irrigation canal networks. Water depth requirement, *gensuishin*, is the measurement of water loss (in millimeters), due to transpiration, total evaporation, and permeation, in a given wet-paddy field per day. A rough estimate of loss during the wet-paddy growing period is approximately 20-25 mm/day, depending on location. Water measurement is not based on absolute volume, but on maintenance of water height in the wet-paddy field. Surface soil puddling, *shirokaki*, is a soil-churning operation that is carried out prior to the transplanting of wet-paddy seedlings while the field is in a waterlogged state. *Shirokaki* prevents water

Social and Economic Features of Japanese Agriculture

The preceding cursory observations about environmental circumstances serve as an essential backdrop to review of the historical, social, and
economic features of the agricultural sector in Japan.   Historically, both
religious values and the political economy of the state have contributed to
the evolution of agricultural land-use patterns.   The Japanese have ab-
stained traditionally from eating meat, as dictated by Buddhist tenets, and
even today caloric intake includes a substantially higher percentage of grains
in comparison to the diet of other developed countries.[14] This cultural
value has a decisive effect on upland agriculture, particularly the development of pastureland, an insignificant feature of the Japanese landscape until
the twentieth century.   The development of lowland areas was influenced
profoundly, however, by the introduction of wet-paddy cultivation in the
second or third century B.C.[15] From that time the cultivation of rice has
been not only the mainstay of Japanese agriculture but a central feature of
the social and economic organization of the state.   One example of its
importance is the fact that harvested rice was the basis of the fiscal system
during the Tokugawa period, 1603 to 1867.   The political and economic
advantages accruing to those in control of increasing yield stimulated
advances in water distribution, flood control, and the identification of high-
yielding seeds responsive to intensive fertilizer use.[16]

---

leakage, simplifies transplanting, mixes fertilizer into the soil, accelerates the breakup of
organic matter, balances the surface of the wet-paddy field, and buries weeds. Midsummer
drainage, *nakaboshi*, is the process of draining the wet-paddy field for a period of seven to
ten days after the initial growth period. Usually taking place in late July/early August, it
improves soil ventilation and promotes root growth. See Latz, *Nihon ni okeru kangai*
[Irrigation in Japan]: 23-32, 43-49. A lucid description of the above procedures can be found in:
Ronald P. Dore, *Shinohata: A Portrait of a Japanese Village* (New York: Pantheon Books,
1978), chapter 6; and Geertz, *Agricultural Involution*: 28-37. The careful definition of
irrigation formulated by Kelly, *Irrigation Management in Japan*: v-vi, is quite useful to
academic research.

[14] Statistics indicate that Japanese consumption of meat, milk, and dairy products is one-
fifth that of the United States. To pick one example, Americans consumed seventy-nine
pounds of beef and veal per capita in 1982, as compared to nine pounds per capita for the
Japanese. Carbohydrates account for 65 percent of caloric intake in Japan, as compared to 43
percent for the United States, an indication of the the high ratio of grains and starchy food in
the Japanese diet. Protein intake also displays an unusual pattern, with approximately one-
half coming from marine products. See Kuroda, "The Present State of Agriculture in Japan":
94-97, 116-17; Okita, "The Proper Approach to Food Policy": 49-57; and United States
Embassy, Tokyo, Japan, "Attache Reports," Foreign Agricultural Service, United States
Department of Agriculture, photocopy.

[15] Good but dated reviews of the history of wet-paddy cultivation in Japan are: Ogasawara,
"The Role of Rice and Rice Paddy Development in Japan": 1-23; and Takane Matsuo, *Rice and*

The steady increase in the arable land base throughout most of the first half of the Tokugawa period had the effect of transforming Japan's lowland agricultural landscape through extensive foreshore and bayhead reclamation of land adjacent to lakes and coastal areas, as well as the filling in of ponds. A geographical characteristic of such agricultural development is the evolution of regional methods of water control like the *kantō ryū*, Kantō River training method, a civil engineering technology for flood prevention and irrigation development initiated in the early seventeenth century in the vicinity of the Tone River.[17] Such water control techniques had a wide-ranging impact on watershed development, particularly expansion of arable land in the eastern part of Saitama prefecture, a feat accomplished, in part, through diversion of the main stem of the Tone River to its present-day outlet near the city of Chōshi, Chiba prefecture. The Ina clan administered the associated flood control and water utilization projects as the special representative for land controlled directly by the central government in Edo (now Tokyo) from the early seventeenth through the eighteenth century. One example dating from this period is the Kasai irrigation canal of Saitama prefecture.

As noted in chapter 1, the development of arable land, either through reclamation or improvement of the existing land base, is a persistent theme in Japanese history. Beginning in the early twentieth century, however, there occurred a shift away from arable land expansion, and since that time a considerable amount of attention has been directed at intensive development of the supporting infrastructure for crop production, especially investment in field replotment, and irrigation and drainage networks (see figures 1, 2, and 3). The intensity of agricultural land use in this century is reflected in yet another way: the existence until the 1930s of a large primary sector, composed of 50 percent or more of the total national labor force.[18] Given

---

Rice Cultivation in Japan (Tokyo: Institute of Asian Economic Affairs, 1961). Also see Itasaka, ed., *Encyclopedia of Japan* 1: 22-24.

[16] Further discussion of the importance of harvested rice to the national economy may be found in: Thomas C. Smith, *The Agrarian Origins of Modern Japan* (Stanford: Stanford University Press, 1959), chapters 7, 8, and 10; Hayami, *Century of Agricultural Growth*: 44-45; and Francks, *Pre-War Agricultural Development*: 28-35.

[17] The pattern of reclamation is discussed generally in Kornhauser, *Japan*: 34-42; and Ogasawara, "The Role of Rice and Rice Paddy Development in Japan": 14-17. Specific comment on regional water-control methods may be found in Latz, *Nihon ni okeru kangai* [Irrigation in Japan]: 55-56.

[18] In 1900 there were 16.6 million people engaged in agriculture, or 68 percent of the labor force. This percentage declined to 50 percent by 1930, totaling 14.7 million people. See Hayami, *Century of Agricultural Growth*: 6-7.

the limited amount of arable land in Japan, this statistic is significant not only in terms of the total number of farmers, but because of what it suggests about the scale of landholdings. For the period 1910 to 1940, for example, between 65 and 71 percent of Japan's approximately 15 million farmers operated holdings less than or equal to one hectare in size.[19] The Japanese agricultural landscape in this century thereby becomes distinctive in two respects: in terms of broadly different land-use patterns in upland and lowland areas; and within lowland areas proper where the scale of agricultural activity reflects the existence of concentrated groups of rural dwellers engaged primarily in wet-paddy cultivation.

A large number of farmers cultivating small plots of land is not only an important lowland landscape feature, but also one of the key socioeconomic characteristics of Japan's land tenure system in the pre-World War II period. A major factor contributing to this situation was the shift, after the Meiji Restoration in 1868, from a subsistence economy to a commodity-based economy. Rising costs of living, declining agricultural prices, and new tax requirements all caused severe problems for the farmer class despite the fact that the production of harvested rice, in terms of yield, rose nearly 50 percent between 1895 and 1940.[20] One ironic statistical indicator of the difficulties experienced by farmers at this time is the estimate that by the mid-1930s approximately 50 percent of the family farm budget was being allocated for food. Their impoverishment made it impossible for most farmers to accumulate capital with which to buy animals or machinery to improve labor productivity or extend the scale of operations, and contributed to the amount of land cultivated by tenant farmers, which increased steadily from the late nineteenth century, reaching a peak of 47 percent by 1930.[21]

Degree of Change in the Agricultural Sector, Post-World War II

Immediately after World War II, a sweeping land reform completely dismantled the landlord-tenant system in Japan.[22] Through programs initi-

---

[19] Fukutake, *Rural Society in Japan:* 4. The figure 15 million for the agricultural labor force is an average for the years mentioned. See Hayami, *Century of Agricultural Growth:* 6-7.

[20] This estimate is based on Ogura, *Can Japanese Agriculture Survive?:* 708. According to this data, average wet-paddy yield at the turn of the century was equal to 2.14 metric tons per hectare; by 1939 it had risen to 3.14 metric tons per hectare.

[21] Fukutake, *Rural Society in Japan:* 15.

[22] The most comprehensive discussion in English of this land transfer program is found in Dore, *Land Reform in Japan.*

ated by the Allied Occupation Forces between 1946 and 1950, over 1.9 million hectares of farmland, one-third of the national total at that time, were redistributed to predominantly independent yeoman farmers.[23] The corresponding effect on tenancy was both direct and immediate. Within four years, by 1950, the amount of land cultivated by tenant farmers was reduced to 10 percent and, concurrently, the number of owner-farmers nearly doubled, shifting from 54 to 90 percent. Agricultural landownership levels stood at 95 percent as of 1975.[24]

Despite these changes in land tenure, efforts to promote enlarged field units, including the enactment of special legislation beginning in 1961, have met with limited success.[25] Statistics indicate that some 70 percent of all farms in Japan continue to be less than or equal to one hectare; average size is 1.2 hectares, and a mere 2 percent of all farms in Japan are larger than three hectares.[26] This phenomenon is quite similar to the pre-World War II landholding pattern, particularly the high percentage of farms less than or equal to one hectare, suggesting the existence of a certain inertia associated with small-scale, family-based cultivation of wet-paddy.

The continuity in the size of land units is especially striking when considered in light of other changes in the post-World War II period, particularly the transformation that has occurred in four respects: degree of mechanization, number of people engaged in full-time agricultural production, income levels of Japanese farmers, and increasing yield of wet-paddy and regional specialization. Each of these interrelated points will be

---

[23] Nōrinsuisanshō Kochika, *Nōchi to kaihō jisseki chōsa* [Survey Results of the Agricultural Land Reform] (Tokyo: Nōrinsuisanshō, 1956). Reproduced in Ogura, *Can Japanese Agriculture Survive?*: 746.

[24] Ogura, *Can Japanese Agriculture Survive?*: 747. It is important to note that at the current time there are few accurate published data on tenancy in Japan. The achievements of the land reform, *nōchi kaikaku*, were protected in 1952 with enactment of the Agricultural Land Law, *Nōchi Hō*, which set severe limits on arable land transfer and the amount of acreage owned by an individual or corporation. A recent trend, however, is an increasing amount of contractual farming, a kind of land tenancy that was stimulated by revision of this law in 1970, and again in 1980. Such deviation from the original policy is at odds with the goal of promoting the establishment of yeoman farmers in Japan but has not been restricted by the Ministry of Agriculture, Forestry and Fisheries since it is compatible with the existing policy programs for enlarging the scale of agricultural production. This point will be discussed further in chapter 3.

[25] To be discussed further in chapter 3 with specific reference to the *Nōgyō Kihon Hō*, Agricultural Basic Law of 1961.

[26] Nōrinsuisanshō, *Pokketo nōrin suisan tōkei, 1983* [Agriculture and Forestry Statistics, 1983, Pocket Edition]: 125, and Kuroda, "Present State of Agriculture in Japan," table 4-A-19, p. 129.

discussed below, concluding with a discussion of continuity and change in the Japanese agricultural sector over the course of the twentieth century.

The transfer of land to private ownership after World War II granted the farmer greater incentive to produce and was accompanied by the adoption of new types of production techniques. The rate at which various aspects of wet-paddy cultivation have become mechanized, from field preparation to crop harvesting, illustrates this point.[27] From 1950 to 1980, for example, gasoline-powered cultivators increased some five-fold, the number in use jumping from 500,000 to over 2.5 million nationwide. More recently, between 1965 and 1980, there has been widespread diffusion of riding tractors, as well as power rice planters and reapers. Explosive growth has occurred especially in the latter two cases, with the total number rising from zero to over 1.5 million units between 1970 and 1980. Perhaps the most important consequence of this mechanization process is a decrease in the amount of time needed for cultivation. In the early twentieth century one-half hectare of wet-paddy required from ninety to a hundred days of labor, including final processing. Since that time, however, there has been an estimated 66 percent reduction in labor requirements, which presently total only thirty to thirty-five days.[28] Most of this decrease in labor demand has occurred in the last twenty years.

Widespread reliance on machinery as a substitute for animal or human labor has a corresponding effect on the number of people needed for crop-production purposes. This has resulted in a significant depopulation of agricultural areas in the post-World War II period, a particularly complex phenomenon in the Japanese case, since total agricultural population has declined at a greater rate than the number of agricultural households. Between 1960 and 1981, for example, the number of persons employed in the farm sector dropped by approximately one-half, slipping from 27 to 10.2 percent of the national labor force, the latter figure equaling approximately 5.6 million people.[29] However, in the same time frame the number of farm households decreased by only about 20 percent, and as of 1982 numbered less than 4.6 million, or some 12 percent of the national household total.[30]

---

[27] For a review of mechanization trends, see Itasaka, ed., *Encyclopedia of Japan* 1: 24-26.

[28] Reduction in labor requirements is discussed in: Kuroda, "Present State of Agriculture in Japan": 102-3, 132; specific reference to wet-paddy cultivation is in Dore, *Shinohata:* 105-6.

[29] Yūjirō Hayami, "Adjustment Policies for Japanese Agriculture in a Changing World," in *U.S.-Japanese Agricultural Trade Relations,* ed. Emery Castle and Kenzō Hemmi (Baltimore: Johns Hopkins University Press, 1982): 377-78.

[30] Nōrinsuisanshō, *Pokketo nōrin suisan tōkei , 1983* [Ministry of Agriculture and Forestry Statistics, 1983, Pocket Edition]: 123.

A number of reasons can be given for this unusual pattern of employment migration. Chief among them is recognition of the general unprofitability of full-time farm employment along with lucrative nonagricultural employment opportunities in the secondary and tertiary sectors of the economy. Beginning in 1960, an increasing percentage of Japan's farmers can be classified as one of two types of part-time farmers, either type one, earning more than half of their income from agricultural pursuits, or type two, where the bulk of income is from nonagricultural sources. By 1982, fully 87 percent of all farmers in Japan can be classified as part-time, with approximately 80 percent in the type-two category.[31] The general pattern is to turn a portion of the farming activities over to the women and grandparents of the household, while the male househead seeks full-time nonagricultural employment in nearby factories or other businesses. When considered in light of the reduced amount of time necessary for wet-paddy production, it is even possible for many so-called farm families to continue cultivating this crop by working as infrequently as each weekend. The progression of part-time farming in the post-World War II period is shown in chart 1.

The popularity of part-time farming in Japan is that it places the farmer in an enviable economic position in terms of both real and potential income. A relatively small amount of labor, for example, garners a high economic return due in large part to a government-supported purchase price for harvested rice that is several times higher than the world market price. The purchase price of harvested rice in Japan, in 1980 equal to 300,050 yen ($1,304) per metric ton, is approximately five times international levels. This resulted in a retail price of approximately 448 yen per kilogram, or eighty-five cents per pound, nearly double the cost of rice in the United States. Government subsidization of Japanese farmers was estimated in 1980 to be nearly $11 billion, equal to 54 percent of total farm income and averaging, by 1981, $2,281 per farmer; half of these subsidies related in one way or another to Japan's rice purchase program. The consumer bears the brunt of these subsidy programs. A 1978 market analysis by the (Japanese) National Institute for Research Advancement concluded that trade restrictions for eight major agricultural products (rice, wheat, barley, potatoes, sugar, milk, beef, and pork) totaled an estimated $16 billion per year.[32]

---

[31] See updated statistics by Japan, Ministry of Agriculture, Forestry and Fisheries, *Abstract of Statistics, 1982*: 67.

[32] However, for the first time in thirty-one years the government's purchase price for rice declined, by 5.95 percent, in 1987. See Latz, "The Persistence of Agriculture in Urban Japan," in press. The role of the government in the marketing of harvested rice can be traced to such policies as the *Beikoku Hō*, Rice Law, 1921, and the World War II *Shokuryō Kanri Seido*, Staple Foodstuff Control System, 1942. For analysis of such government programs, a field of study unto itself, see: Attache Reports, Foreign Agricultural Service, United States Depart-

In addition to the subsidization support, there are also certain tax and loan advantages for the farmer that, combined with the rising price of farmland since 1975, probably guarantee economic security upon retirement and certainly create a nouveau riche class through land sell-off. The price of agricultural land in Japan skyrocketed in the period between 1960 and 1980 owing to rapid economic growth and the oil shock of 1973. Statistics indicate that land prices increased at an average annual rate of 17 to 20 percent in rural areas, and 27 percent in urban areas. The effect of such inflation is that there is greater incentive to hold land as an asset. The average price of agricultural land approached 30 million yen per hectare (approximately $130,000) in 1980.[33]

In contrast to the poverty of the prewar period and to the adverse circumstances which existed even during national economic recovery immediately after World War II, the present-day standard of living enjoyed by farmers compares favorably with that of urban dwellers and particularly other blue-collar laborers in Japan. Even as recently as the 1960s, average farm income trailed behind the urban wage earner's income by 11 percent on a per household basis, and 32 percent on a per capita basis.[34] By 1975, however, per capita farm household income had moved ahead, and, of greater significance, average farm household income in 1982 was approximately 23 percent higher than average blue-collar household income nationwide.[35] This changed state of affairs seems to have had the most positive effect on part-time farmers whose agricultural incomes are supplemental and who own small amounts of farmland, less than one hectare. This group, representing 80 percent of all farm households and controlling 44 percent of all cultivated land, now has an extraordinarily high average

---

ment of Agriculture, 1980-84, including United States Embassy, Tokyo, "Attache Reports"; Coyle, "Japan's Rice Policy"; Ravenholt, "The Japanese Farmer"; Ogura, *Can Japanese Agriculture Survive?:* chapter 3; Castle and Hemmi, eds., *U.S.-Japanese Agricultural Trade Relations:* chapters 3-5 and 10-11; and Michael W. Donnelly, "Conflict over Government Authority and Markets: Japan's Rice Economy," in *Conflict in Japan,* ed. Ellis Krauss et al. (Honolulu: University of Hawaii Press, 1984): 355-74. Note: for 1980 statistics, $1 equals 230 yen; for 1982 statistics, $1 equals 200 yen.

[33] See Kuroda, "Present State of Agriculture in Japan": 100-101, 128; and Fumio Egaitsu, "Japanese Agricultural Policy," in *U.S.-Japanese Agricultural Trade Relations,* ed. Emery Castle and Kenzō Hemmi (Baltimore: Johns Hopkins University Press, 1982): 172, 180.

[34] Hayami, "Adjustment Policies for Japanese Agriculture": 381-82.

[35] United States Embassy, Tokyo, "Attache Reports," 1984. The 1982 average annual income for farm households was 6.2 million yen, approximately $31,000.

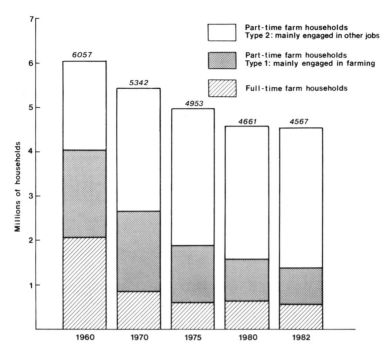

Chart 1. Number of farm households in Japan, 1960-82.
Adapted from Ministry of Agriculture, Forestry and Fisheries, *Abstract of Statistics, Japan/ 1982*, 1983: 2.

income and a large amount of disposable income compared to other farmers.[36]

The relationship between part-time farming and the relatively high incomes of farmers in Japan is often discussed in the literature as a by-product of rapid growth in the secondary and tertiary sectors of the economy.[37] However, these external conditions should not obscure one of the great achievements of the Japanese agricultural sector, the overall increase both in the total production of wet-paddy and in the average yield per hectare in the post-World War II period. Production is estimated to have expanded by more than 50 percent between 1950 and 1975, from 8.6 to 13.2

[36] This observation is based on analyses by: Hayami, "Adjustment Policies for Japanese Agriculture": 169-70, 174; and Egaitsu, "Japanese Agricultural Policy": 380. This research confirms that part-time farmers whose income from agriculture is supplemental are most heavily committed to wet-paddy cultivation.

[37] Thoughtful and perspicacious comments about the relationship between the agricultural sector and the rest of the Japanese economy can be found in Dore, *Shinohata:* 109 and 312-18.

million metric tons, and average yield per hectare during this period increased 45 percent, from 3.3 to 4.8 metric tons.[38] These increases have been
accompanied by significant shifts in the geographical distribution of wet-
paddy production in the post-World War II period, with the high productivity centers migrating from the regions of Kinki and south central Chūbu
to northwest Chūbu (Hokuriku) and Tōhoku.[39] Such adjustments are due
primarily to the creation of hybrid seeds capable of maturation in growing
environments with shorter and cooler summers typical of north-central and
northeastern Japan.[40] By the late 1960s and early 1970s these areas had
become much more efficient in both land and labor productivity, while the
traditional rice bowl of Japan, the Kinki region, had diversified its
agricultural activity to include production of horticultural products, beef,
poultry, and swine. Two other examples of regional specialization should
be noted: the migration of vegetable, beef, and poultry producers to sites
near urban centers, and a concentration of fruit production in selected parts
of Kyūshū, Chūbu, and Tōhoku.

Even as wet-paddy yield was increasing, however, per capita consumption of rice in the post-World War II period began to decline as the
Japanese diet came to include greater amounts of wheat, dairy products,
meat, and other so-called Western foods. (See chart 2). Concurrently, there
was a dramatic decline in double-cropping ratios, from 134 to 104 between
1960 and 1977, as farmers took advantage of lucrative nonagricultural jobs.[41]
It is worth noting, with regard to this trend, that part-time farm households
with the smallest units of production show the highest degree of specialization in wet-paddy cultivation. Thus, part-time farmers whose agricultural income is supplemental "are more and more inclined to rely only
on production of rice . . . because distribution of rice is under government

---

[38] Itasaka, ed., *Encyclopedia of Japan* 1: 25; and Sanderson, *Japan's Food Prospects and Policies:* 6-9. Average yield in 1980 stood at 4.1 metric tons per hectare; see Nōrinsuisanshō Kōzōkaizenkyoku Kensetsubu Sekkeika, ed., *Tochi kairyō yōran* [Summary of Land Improve-ment] (Tokyo: Nōrinsuisanshō Kōzōkaizenkyoku Kensetsubu Sekkeika, 1981): 84-85. See also Keith Brown, "Agriculture in Japan: The Crisis of Success," *Japan Society Newsletter* (Sept. 1986): 2-5.

[39] See Ebato, *Postwar Japanese Agriculture:* 17-21, figures 13.1, 13.2; and Motosuke Ishii, "Regional Trends in the Changing Agrarian Structure of Postwar Japan," in *Geography of Japan*, ed. Association of Japanese Geographers, Special Publication no. 4 (Tokyo: Teikoku-Shoin Co., 1980): 194-222. See also map 1.

[40] Wet-paddy technology and the development of hybrid seeds are discussed in Hayami, *Century of Agricultural Growth:* 117-31.

[41] Kuroda, "Present State of Agriculture in Japan": 100.

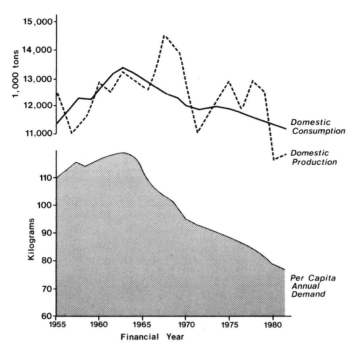

Chart 2. Supply of and demand for rice in Japan, 1955-81.
Adapted from Singh and Shōgo Yuihama, "Recent Structural Transformation of Japanese Agriculture": 209.

control [and] there is no marketing problem . . . or risk because prices are officially guaranteed."[42]

As self-sufficiency ratios in many commodities other than harvested rice declined, the shortfall in local production of such crops as wheat, barley, soybeans, and feed grains could be balanced only through additional, selective importation from the United States, Canada, and Brazil. Between 1960 and 1977, Japanese self-sufficiency ratios for wheat dropped from 39 to 4 percent, for barley from 107 to 9 percent, for soybeans from 28 to 3 percent,

---

[42] Egaitsu, "Japanese Agricultural Policy": 174. Hayami expands on this point: "Because rice marketing is carried out exclusively by the government, rice farmers are guaranteed a high price and can easily sell their harvest through agricultural cooperatives, the sole agents of government rice marketing. In addition, agricultural research and extension services have traditionally concentrated on the rice crop to the extent that rice cultivation has become highly standardized and there is little difference in productivity between part-time and full-time farmers. The fact that the production of Japan's staple crop has been geared to part-time farming in this way is thus a major factor encouraging part-time farming and impeding any decline in the number of farm-households." Hayami, "Adjustment Policies for Japanese Agriculture": 379-81.

and for feed grains from 66 to 2 percent. Between 1977 and 1982, these commodities, with the exception of feed grains, rebounded to 12, 15, and 5 percent, respectively. Japan is the largest overseas market for American agricultural goods, importing $8.2 billion of agriculturally related commodities, consumer items, and forestry products in 1983. This is equal to 15 percent of total U.S. farm exports. The United States supplied 95 percent of all imported soybeans and 59 percent of all imported wheat to Japan in 1977; altogether, one out of twenty acres cultivated in the United States produces agricultural products for the Japanese market, an acreage larger than the total amount of cropland in Japan.[43]

In short, Japan's program for increasing production of wet-paddy land became so successful that overproduction of harvested rice reached a crisis stage in the late 1960s. Harvested rice production peaked at 14.5 million metric tons in 1967; by 1969 Japan was producing nearly 2.5 million metric tons of harvested rice in excess of demand. Demand, in contrast, peaked in 1962 at 118 kilograms per capita, and stood at 76.4 kilograms per capita in 1982.

Since the early 1970s, attempts have been made to implement a diversification policy for agriculture that restricts wet-paddy cultivation on approximately 570,000 hectares and accounts for a decline in total production over the past decade of roughly 3 million metric tons.[44] This production drop reflects the difficulties inherent in managing a government policy that overemphasized self-sufficiency in one commodity when contemporary circumstances required a diversified agricultural base to meet consumer demands. A central factor influencing this supply-and-demand problem, as noted earlier, is the fact that the market purchase price for harvested rice is controlled artificially by the government at a rate several times the world level, which in turn encourages overspecialization in wet-paddy cultivation

---

[43] See United States Embassy, Tokyo, "Attache Reports," 1980-84; Fred Sanderson, "Managing Our Agricultural Interdependence," *U.S.-Japanese Agricultural Trade Relations*, ed. Emery Castle and Kenzō Hemmi (Baltimore: Johns Hopkins University Press, 1982): 393-426; Itasaka, ed., *Encyclopedia of Japan* 1: 31.

[44] In 1982 harvested rice production equaled 9.35 million metric tons. In 1970, in contrast, total production equaled 12.5 million metric tons. See Japan, Ministry of Agriculture, Forestry and Fisheries, Statistics and Information Department, *Crop Statistics* (annual) (Tokyo: Ministry of Agriculture, Forestry and Fisheries, 1982). A discussion of diversification policy can be found in Donnelly, "Conflict over Government Authority and Markets": 362-64; and Sanderson, "Managing Our Agricultural Interdependence": 416-17. It should be noted that the costs of the crop diversification program are extremely high and exceeded $2 billion dollars as of 1980. Ironically, this attempt to diversify Japan's production base has been more expensive than continuation of the program for wet-paddy cultivation. See Sanderson, p. 417. Review of terminology for production adjustment, *seisan chōsei*, can be found in Latz, *Nihon ni okeru kangai* [Irrigation in Japan]: 41.

by Japanese farmers. National concern about self-sufficiency in the production of this particular commodity has had a significant influence on the evolution of this policy. Chapter 3 will discuss further several of the legislative decisions that have shaped post-World War II Japanese agricultural policy, including attempts to stabilize urban and rural incomes during the period of rapid economic growth in the 1960s.

Two interrelated themes emerge from this review of Japan's primary sector. The first is the complex relationship between wet-paddy cultivation, the location of such agricultural production, and the crucial importance of water supply to high yield. A second concerns the degree of both continuity and change in contemporary Japanese agriculture.[45] Over the past eighty years, for example, the scale of farm units has remained virtually constant at about one hectare, whereas socioeconomic circumstances have been altered radically. From a policy perspective, it can be argued, these two observations represent the complex environmental, social, and economic conditions that development programs have had to contend with. In the chapter to follow

---

[45] This observation about continuity and change is well illustrated through comparison of the main characteristics of Japanese agriculture in the pre- and post-World War II periods. In the prewar period the agricultural sector was characterized by a high percentage of the labor force, increasing rates of tenancy, and a shift from an expanding to a relatively stable arable land base manipulated with increasing intensity, resulting in higher wet-paddy yield. The post-World War II period differs dramatically. First, there was a wholesale transfer of landownership rights by means of the land reform, followed by a contraction of the arable land base and the farming population. At the present time there is less intensive land use on a year-round basis, but greater specialization in wet-paddy cultivation. The main examples of radical change in the postwar period are: mechanization, part-time farming, agricultural incomes, and wet-paddy yield. Viewed either in terms of the twentieth century as a whole, or in terms of the roughly forty years before and after World War II, agricultural areas in Japan have gone through a remarkable transformation. Despite the degree of change that dominates this commentary on the primary sector, however, it should also be noted that in certain respects Japanese agriculture exhibits equally remarkable continuity in the midst of change. This observation is reflected first and foremost by the fact that the physical size of farm units has remained virtually constant throughout the twentieth century, averaging approximately one hectare. In addition, the gross amount of arable land and the percentage of it devoted to wet-paddy cultivation have been relatively static, at least until 1960 when Japan entered a period of very rapid economic growth. A final example of continuity is that there has been a steady increase in wet-paddy yield through the entire twentieth century. When the latter view of continuity is compared with that of change, the picture of the Japanese agricultural sector becomes paradoxical. How is it, for example, that yield increases despite the fixed scale of production units and a decline in both the total amount of agricultural land under production and the percentage of the agricultural labor force engaged in full-time farming? The answer to this question is severalfold, and includes technological achievements in the development and dissemination of hybrid seeds, as well as the application of modern engineering techniques to reshape agricultural producing sites so that the degree of water control is elevated to the extent that high-yielding hybrid seeds can be introduced successfully. Chapter 3 examines this point.

the characteristics of Japanese agricultural policy for improving production of wet-paddy will be examined in more detail, with particular emphasis on investment programs for the land infrastructure, and water distribution and drainage networks.

Chapter 3

POLICIES FOR AGRICULTURAL
INFRASTRUCTURE DEVELOPMENT

Evaluation of the role of government policy in the development of the Japanese agricultural sector presents a number of definitional problems. One of these is the need to distinguish between policies that directly and indirectly influence the physical development of crop-producing sites. The primary observation in chapter 2, that the physical scale of farm units has remained virtually constant in this century, averaging approximately one hectare in size, illustrates this point. It is now widely accepted that contemporary government policies have contributed to this pattern of agricultural development. Two reasons are commonly given to explain why farmland has not become concentrated, leading to scale expansion, since World War II. The primary reason is the rapid economic growth and the high percentage of part-time farmers in Japan, the vast majority of whom earn most of their income outside the agricultural sector. A second major reason for small-scale farming stems from agricultural policies; two examples worthy of particular emphasis are the Agricultural Land Law, *Nōchi Hō*, and the Staple Foodstuff Control System, *Shokuryō Kanri Seido*. The former policy had the effect, at least until the 1970s, of restricting farmland ownership to 3.5 hectares in an attempt to prevent a revival of landlordism.[1] The latter policy, by fixing the price of harvested rice at an artificially inflated level, grants the farmer a high economic return on intermittent labor without requiring a corresponding increase in the size of the arable land unit.

Each of these policies, like rapid economic growth, has a clear-cut, negative influence on scale expansion, encouraging part-time agricultural

---

[1] The figure applies to all areas except Hokkaidō, where the maximum amount is higher.

activity while stymieing the transfer of farmland to full-time farmers seeking to acquire larger parcels. However, policies that reinforce small-scale agriculture by restricting the amount of land an individual may own, or by manipulating the market for a given commodity, are not representative of efforts by the Japanese government to invest directly in the agricultural infrastructure. The purpose of this chapter, therefore, is to identify the main characteristics of agricultural infrastructure development programs in Japan, with specific reference to post-World War II policy for land improvement, *tochi kairyō seisaku*. The institutional features of this policy will be the main object of analysis, particularly operation of the *Tochi Kairyō Ku*, Land Improvement District (henceforth abbreviated as LID or "district" wherever possible), the administrative unit responsible for channeling infrastructure investment at the field level.

The foundation for the discussion to follow was set in place in chapter 1, with its cursory definition of land improvement policy as an attempt to encourage more intensive use of existing farmland through government-subsidized civil engineering projects for the purpose of either reforming or developing the infrastructure for crop production. In this chapter the evolution of this policy in the twentieth century will be reviewed in greater detail. As in chapter 1, terminology definition will be stressed,[2] as will the graphic illustration of changes in the pattern of land and water use due to infrastructure investment. My conclusions will guide case-study analysis of the LID in chapter 4.

Land Improvement Policy: A Tentative Definition

Review of the Japanese literature for agricultural development indicates that the term "land improvement," *tochi kairyō*, has at least three different, though related, meanings.[3] First, it refers specifically to the upgrading of the arable land infrastructure in the post-World War II period, including farmland consolidation, and the construction or renovation of irrigation and drainage canals, weirs, headworks, and water-warming facilities.[4] A second, broader definition is based on the objectives stated in

---

[2] See also Latz, *Nihon ni okeru kangai* [Irrigation in Japan], especially pp. 33-42.

[3] As noted in chapter 1, this legislative term can be traced to the *Tochi Kairyō Hō*, Land Improvement Law (no. 195), in 1949 (Showa 24). An important precedent to this legislation is the *Kōchi Seiri Hō*, Arable Land Reorganization Law (no. 82), in 1899 (Meiji 32). See chapter 1, note 8, for a listing of the primary references for this section.

[4] Because of the highly specialized meaning of irrigation terminology in the Japanese literature, I shall define each of these terms. (1) Farmland consolidation, *hojō seibi:* those land improvement projects which increase productivity of dry-field or wet-paddy agriculture through consolidation of the agricultural infrastructure. Specifically, this includes land

the Land Improvement Law of 1949, *Tochi Kairyō Hō*, including programs for land development, land reclamation, and natural disaster protection.[5] Third, the term is used most generally to refer to all activities related to the

---

exchange and consolidation, soil dressing, subsoil compaction, pipeline irrigation facilities, and underdrainage development. Such facility reorganization does not normally extend beyond an individual field unit proper, and therefore does not include mainline irrigation and drainage projects. A related term is *kukaku seiri*, land readjustment. The following points should be emphasized regarding differences between these two terms: (a) farmland consolidation is a comprehensive approach for reorganization of the agricultural field with emphasis on both the reshaping of land parcels and pipeline irrigation or underdrainage at the site level; (b) land readjustment, in contrast, has a much narrower objective which concentrates on the shape of land parcels only, and may refer to nonagricultural land development. Both types of development are guided chiefly by a land-planning criterion that aims at establishing land units 30 *āru* (30 x 100 meters) in size, the so-called *hyōjun kukaku*, standard farmland block; the post-World War II goal of promoting mechanization of agriculture, especially since the 1960s, is based on such standardization of land units. See figures 1, 2, and 3, and chart 3. (2) Irrigation canals, modern, *yōsui ro*: structures that conduct irrigation water. In terms of construction and function, the following three distinctions should be noted: (a) those canals connected directly to the water source, or main (trunk) canals, *kansen yōsui ro*; (b) those that branch off the main canal, or branch (submain) canals, *shisen yōsui ro*; (c) and those that run directly adjacent to arable land parcels, or ditch (subbranch) canals, *saisho yōsui ro*. (3) Drainage canals, modern, *haisui ro*: a canal that gathers and drains excess water due to rain, residual water from irrigation, or inflow of water from outside the immediate area of cultivation. Types include: (a) main drainage canals, *kansen haisui ro*; (b) branch (submain) drainage canals, *shisen haisui ro*; (c) lateral drainage canals, *shohaisui ro*. (4) Weir, *seki*: a dam-like structure which raises the level of marshes, lakes, rivers, or irrigation canals for the purpose of water intake. Also used to regulate water quantity. Weirs can be classified according to: (a) structure, including fixed weirs, *kotei zeki*, and movable weirs, *kadō zeki*; (b) function, such as diversion weirs, *shusui zeki*; or (c) angle of construction, such as slanted weirs, *naname seki*. (5) Headworks, *tōshukō*: a facility for drawing needed water from lakes, marshes, or rivers. In order to control the inflow rate this structure is normally composed of diversion weirs and intakes. The term "headworks" may be used synonymously with "gravity-type irrigation intake facilities," *shizen ryūka gata shusui shisetsu;* the distinction between the two, however, is that the former refers to the intake and water gate (weir) only, while the latter is a more sophisticated structure, sometimes controlled by a complex computer system, and may include a portion of the irrigation canal proper. (6) Water warming facilities, *onsui shisetsu*: engineering facilities established to guard against damage caused by low water temperature, including water warming canals, *onsui ro*, and water warming ponds, *onsui ike*. A related facility is the detour waterway, *mawashi suiro*; this facility, in order to prevent crop injury due to low water temperature at the irrigation inlet to the wet-paddy field, does not conduct water directly into the field, but guides it slowly through a winding channel where land and air temperatures act as moderating agents. See Latz, *Nihon ni okeru kangai* [Irrigation in Japan]: 23-32, 43-49, and 65-79 for further discussion and illustration of the terminology noted above.

[5] Agricultural land development, *nōyōchi kaihatsu*, refers to the conversion of virgin land or waste land to agricultural use; development of the upper reaches of alluvial fans is one example. Protection of agricultural lands susceptible to natural disasters, *nōchi bosai hozen*, refers to construction of facilities that protect existing farmland from natural disasters caused by torrential rain, earthquakes, or related natural catastrophes. See Okabe, *Zusetsu tochi kairyō 100 kō* [100 Lectures on Land Improvement]: 18-33.

development of arable land or water control facilities established from the late nineteenth through the twentieth century. The last meaning is the least precise, since the pre-World War II legislation for infrastructure investment, i.e., the Arable Land Reorganization Law of 1899, *Kōchi Seiri Hō*,[6] represents a program for agricultural development that was not necessarily the same as that found in the 1949 law. This important point can be clarified by reviewing briefly the characteristics of these policies for agricultural development; particular emphasis will be placed on the post-World War II period.[7]

Kōchi Seiri Hō: Arable Land Reorganization Law of 1899

The Arable Land Reorganization Law, enacted in 1899, had as its primary objective the grouping of scattered landholdings in order to promote more efficient use of labor, water, and other inputs for wet-paddy production. This goal was to be accomplished through establishment of a legal framework authorizing Arable Land Reorganization Associations, *Kōchi Seiri Kumiai,* to promote projects for land exchange and consolidation, *kokan bungō;* farm lot adjustment, *denku kaisei;* land reclamation (including conversion of farmland from dry-field to wet-paddy agriculture), *kaikon;* and construction of irrigation and drainage facilities, *yōhaisui shisetsu.*[8] Projects for such infrastructure investment were characterized by a coercive element; should two-thirds of the landowners in a given area support the project, all beneficiaries would be required to participate.[9]

---

[6] The *Kōchi Seiri Hō* is also translated as the Arable Land Replotment Law, the Arable Land Consolidation Law, the Cultivated Land Readjustment Law, and the Arable Land Readjustment Law. The term "reorganization" seems most appropriate, however, given the objectives of this legislation, as discussed in this chapter, below.

[7] This review is based on course work at the University of Tokyo, Institute of Human Geography, 1980-83. General usage of land improvement terminology is reviewed and critiqued in: Shibata, "Nōgyō suiri no shisutemu" [Agricultural Water-Use System]: 65-67; and Shibata, "Saitama ken minumadai yōsui ni okeru nōgyō suiri shisutemu" [Agricultural Water-Use System in Minumadai Canal of Saitama Prefecture]: 1-2.

[8] The language of this policy is discussed further in Latz, *Nihon ni okeru kangai* [Irrigation in Japan]: 25, 33, 48, and 51.

[9] Precisely speaking, in the original Arable Land Reorganization Law, *Kōchi Seiri Hō,* the shouldering of project costs was compulsory if two-thirds of the landowners, representing two-thirds of the total land value affected, voted to participate. In the revision of 1909, however, only one-half the landowners had to agree to project implementation. In addition, small landowner consent, representing 16.6 percent of all landowners, was no longer necessary. See Shibata, "Nōgyō suiri no shisutemu" [Agricultural Water-Use System]: 68-69.

The legal authority of the Arable Land Reorganization Association, to function as an administrative vehicle for carrying out such agricultural development, was reinforced by legislative revisions in 1909. These revisions were significant in three respects:[10] they heralded a shift in emphasis from farmland replotment to irrigation and drainage projects; they clarified the legal authority of the Arable Land Reorganization Association to collect levies from participating farmers through the tax system, which had the effect of reducing financial risk through greater reliance on public and private institutions of credit; and they distinguished clearly between infrastructure investment organizations, like the Arable Land Reorganization Association, and irrigation facility maintenance organizations, like the Regular Water-Use Association, *Fūtsu Suiri Kumiai*, the latter previously established in 1890 by the Regular Water-Use Association Law, *Fūtsu Suiri Kumiai Hō*.[11] Participation in such organizations as the Arable Land Reorganization Association and the Regular Water-Use Association was limited to landowners.

Although the original intent of the Arable Land Reorganization Law, *Kōchi Seiri Hō*, was to emphasize projects for grouping of scattered landholdings in order to increase agricultural production, it should be underscored that revisions subsequent to 1909, the date of the so-called new law, had the effect of shifting attention to projects for water supply, distribution, and drainage. This change was reinforced in 1923, with the promulgation of the Rules for Subsidization of Irrigation and Drainage Projects, *Yōhaisui Kairyō Jigyō Hojo Yōkō*, authorizing the central government to provide subsidies of 50 percent to prefectural governments if the proposed water-control project was to affect an area greater than 500 hectares.

The increasing degree of public involvement in infrastructure development during the pre-World War II period is reflected by the ratio of government investment to total investment, estimated to have gone from 22 to 40 percent between the early 1900s and the late 1930s; the total area

---

10 See Ibid.: 68-71.

11 The purpose of the Regular Water-Use Association Law, *Fūtsu Suiri Kumiai Hō*, was to establish a legal framework for maintenance of irrigation facilities. This objective was accomplished through creation of the Regular Water-Use Association, *Fūtsu Suiri Kumiai*, a legally established organization for collecting maintenance-related monies whose origin can be traced to the 1890 Ordinance for Water-Use Associations, *Suiri Kumiai Jōrei*. Two points should be emphasized about the Regular Water-Use Association: (1) in contrast to the development activities of the Arable Land Reorganization Association, *Kōchi Seiri Kumiai*, operation focused on maintenance of existing irrigation networks; and (2) the newly established boundaries for these associations differed from those of the traditional municipalities, which, in many cases, had evolved originally from customary water-use practices, *suiri kankō*. See Latz, *Nihon ni okeru kangai* [Irrigation in Japan]: 33-34.

benefiting from infrastructure monies during this same time is estimated to
have been 1.4 million hectares, or 23 percent of all arable land as of 1940.
The annual level of government expenditure immediately prior to World
War II equaled 30 million yen. The regions of highest investment were:
Tōhoku, 22.6 percent, and Kyūshū, 15.8 percent; regions of lowest investment were Kinki, 6.8 percent, and Chūgoku, 8.3 percent. Regional investment trends reflect the attempt by the national government to adjust the
infrastructure and encourage more intensive agricultural production.[12]

Tochi Kairyō Hō: Land Improvement Law of 1949

The Land Improvement Law of 1949, while based on legal precedents
and objectives found in the 1899 legislation and its revisions, differs in
several respects, most notably by allowing the participation of both tenants
and landowners, and emphasizing more comprehensive infrastructure investment.[13] Of particular interest is the expanding range and total number
of infrastructure investment projects, which include not only development
or refurbishing of irrigation and drainage facilities, yōhaisui shisetsu; land
reclamation, kaikon; and (farm) land readjustment, kukaku seiri; but
farmland consolidation, hojō seibi, village consolidation, nōson seibi, farm
road consolidation, nōdō seibi; and agricultural water-use rationalization,
nōgyō yōsui gōrika.[14] If all types of projects for land improvement are

---

[12] These investment patterns are based on the research of: Hayami, Century of Agricultural
Growth: 172, 174-79, 226-27, and 235; and Francks, Pre-War Agricultural Development: 80-81.
Calculated in terms of the inflationary period of 1941, total investment equaled nearly 8.5
billion yen. See also map 1.

[13] The comprehensive nature of land improvement policy is reflected by the number of
projects that qualify for subsidization from government financial organs. There are ten main
categories of projects: irrigation and drainage, kangai haisui; farmland consolidation, hojō
seibi; agricultural road consolidation, nōdō seibi; comprehensive land improvement of dry
field zones, hatake chitai sōgō tochi kairyō; comprehensive village consolidation, nōson sōgō
seibi; protection of agricultural lands susceptible to disasters, nōchi bōsai hozen; agricultural
land development, nōyōchi kaihatsu; damaged land rehabilitation, saigai fukyū; land
improvement facilities for maintenance control, tochi kairyō shisetsu iji kanri; and other
types of land improvement, sho tochi kairyō. See: Okabe, Zusetsu tochi kairyō 100 kō [100
Lectures on Land Improvement]: 22-23; Shibata, "Nōgyō suiri no shisutemu" [Agricultural
Water-Use System]: 65; Shibata, "Saitama ken minumadai yōsui ni okeru nōgyō suiri
shisutemu" [Agricultural Water-Use System of Minumadai Canal of Saitama Prefecture]: 1-2;
Nōrinsuisanshō, Tochi kairyō no zenyō [Comprehensive Summary of Land Improvement],
1982: 13-19; Imamura Naraomi, Hojokin to nōgyō, nōson [Villages, Agriculture, and Subsidies]
(Tokyo: Ie no Hikari Kyōkai, 1982): 159-94.

[14] Comprehensive village consolidation, nōson sōgō seibi, is a new land improvement
category that is not necessarily related to upgrading of the agricultural production system,
and may include the construction of recreation facilities in a given village. The evolution of
land improvement policy to include the social infrastructure, and the rapid expansion in the

considered, the number now totals nearly 400; some eighty of these are directly related to the main objectives of the LID, *Tochi Kairyō Ku*, the legally established administrative body responsible for cost-sharing negotiations between the government and farmers participating in infrastructure investment projects. As stipulated by the 1949 legislation, the LID assumes the maintenance and developmental objectives of the previously existing Arable Land Reorganization Associations, *Kōchi Seiri Kumiai*, and the Regular Water-Use Associations, *Fūtsu Suiri Kumiai*. The same type of coercive participation requirements found in the early twentieth-century legislation are retained.[15]

The environmental and socioeconomic features of the primary sector suggest the kind of development problems that land improvement policy must contend with at the site of crop production. Infrastructure investment projects associated with wet-paddy cultivation, the dominant crop in the mix of agricultural land uses in Japan, can be used as a representative example. Successful production assumes four conditions in the Japanese case: adequate supplies of water throughout the cultivation period; an irrigation network for water transfer from source to site of demand; a drainage network for timely removal of surplus water at specified periods during the cultivation cycle and immediately prior to harvest; and some kind of cooperative organization capable of managing irrigation and drainage networks.[16] Figures 2 and 3 compare graphically the characteristic

---

types of post-World War II LIDs, will be considered in separate research. The reader should note that terminology describing infrastructure investment changes after 1949, i.e., *kōchi seiri*, has been superseded by the terms *tochi kairyō, hojō seibi*, and *kukaku seiri*, although the latter two are not equal in importance to *tochi kairyō* and, in fact, are contained within a definition of it.

[15] Enactment of the Land Improvement Law, *Tochi Kairyō Hō*, led to the dissolution, in 1952, of the Regular Water-Use Association, *Fūtsu Suiri Kumiai*, and the Arable Land Reorganization Association, *Kōchi Seiri Kumiai*.

[16] The statement above is, admittedly, a rather rough definition of the prerequisite conditions for successful wet-paddy cultivation. The primary concern of this chapter, however, is less with formal definitions of wet-paddy production, and the concomitant problem of water control, than with a comprehensible review of policy for such agricultural activity. As noted elsewhere, there are methodological problems when equating irrigation network development with land improvement projects; the latter clearly have a broader set of responsibilities, which include farmland consolidation, *hojō seibi*; comprehensive village consolidation, *nōson sōgō seibi*; and farm road consolidation, *nōdō seibi*; as well as construction or renovation of irrigation and drainage facilities, *kangai yōhaisui shisetsu*. See Latz, *Nihon ni okeru kangai* [Irrigation in Japan]: 1-6. Thus, whereas an appropriate definition of irrigation may refer to "the entire cycle of agricultural water use," this is not to say that LIDs are essentially irrigation groupings. See Kelly, *Irrigation Management in Japan*: v-vi, 15. To argue that the LID is essentially an irrigation grouping misinterprets the role these administrative units play in the development of the primary sector. In short, while it is true that the actual boundaries of the district may correspond to the traditional zone of irrigation,

features of wet-paddy cultivation before and after the turn of the century and the ways in which infrastructure investment has altered the pattern of land and water use at the field level.

A composite sketch of the traditional agricultural landscape is depicted in figure 2. The field layout, irregular with individual plots varying in size, reflects the small scale and scattered nature of traditional agricultural activity in Japan.[17] Typically, irrigation and drainage are combined in one canal; this has the effect of restricting water control regionally and at the individual field level. Within the fields proper, the irrigation network does not distribute water to separate land units, relying instead on overland flow, or plot-to-plot irrigation, *tagoshi kangai*.[18] A high degree of cooperation between adjoining cultivators is required for water distribution. Road access to each field is extremely limited, suggesting the complex problems associated with attempts to introduce machinery related to the cultivation process.

---

their function is not necessarily limited to irrigation activity. To conclude otherwise fails to consider contemporary socioeconomic changes in the agricultural sector. This point is discussed further in chapter 4.

[17] Although the sketches are designed to represent the changes accompanying infrastructure investment policy before and after World War II, it should be emphasized that a typical prewar landscape may have been reordered based on the Arable Land Reorganization Law, *Kōchi Seiri Hō*. It is important to keep in mind, however, the general absence of widespread, large-scale replotment or mechanized pumping in the pre-World War II period. Infrastructure investment, when it did occur, concentrated on the combination of irrigation and drainage canals, as stipulated by the 1909 revisions to the Arable Land Reorganization Law. In contrast, postwar investment had a much more discernible effect, particularly farmland consolidation projects, *hojō seibi jigyō*, leading to the rearrangement of fields at a larger scale of 30 *āru*, including pump irrigation facilities where required, as qualified by note 4, above. Additional illustration of twentieth-century changes in the Japanese agricultural landscape can be found in Latz, *Nihon ni okeru kangai* [Irrigation in Japan]: 65-79.

[18] Plot-to-plot irrigation, *tagoshi kangai*, is a traditional irrigation method in which water comes in contact with only the upper portion of a particular arable land parcel. Water flows from the irrigation canal into the wet-paddy field at this uppermost point and is then distributed to adjoining fields; not every field division comes into direct contact with the irrigation canal. This method is characteristic of premodern water distribution techniques. Particularly after the *nōchi kaikaku*, land reform (1946-50), rationalization of water use led to the goal of distributing water to each individual holding of the new class of independent yeoman farmers. An equivalent term is *kake nagashi*. Plot-to-plot irrigation should not be confused with continuous irrigation, *renzoku kangai*. The latter is an irrigation method that circulates water continuously atop arable land and involves careful maintenance of water depth. Limitations of this technique are insufficient control of water temperature and loss of soil nutrients due to soil erosion. The practice may be distinguished from plot-to-plot irrigation in that continuous irrigation refers to a cultivation method rather than to the movement of water between fields. Plot-to-plot irrigation is illustrated in Latz, *Nihon ni okeru kangai* [Irrigation in Japan]: 73.

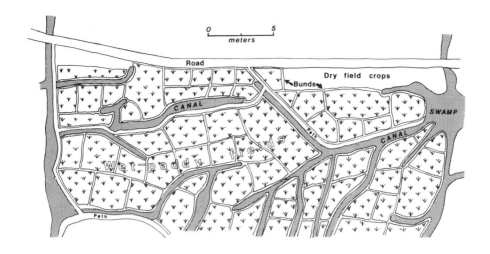

Fig. 2. *Pattern of land and water use in wet-paddy areas, traditional.*
Adapted from Latz, *Nihon ni okeru kangai*: 72. Original source: Japanese Society of Irrigation, Drainage, and Reclamation Engineering, ed., *Irrigation and Drainage in Japan Pictorial*: 56.

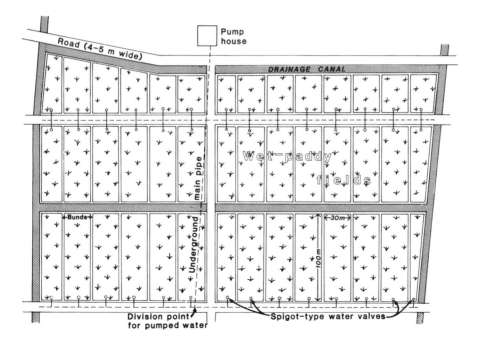

Fig. 3. *Pattern of land and water use in wet-paddy areas, modern.*
Adapted from Latz, *Nihon ni okeru kangai*: 75. Original source: Japanese Society of Irrigation, Drainage, and Reclamation Engineering, ed., *Irrigation and Drainage in Japan Pictorial*: 70.

The traditional pattern of agricultural land and water use may be contrasted to figure 3, a composite sketch isolating land improvement policy objectives in the post-World War II period. Here the application of civil engineering techniques results in a remarkable transformation of the agricultural landscape. Farmland is grouped into larger-scale rectangular parcels, 30 x 100 meters in size (30 *āru* or .3 hectares), a prerequisite to the efficient use of machinery for crop cultivation and harvesting. Dual-purpose canals are constructed which separate facilities for irrigation and drainage, allowing for greater control over water distribution. In the wet-paddy field proper, pipeline irrigation facilities have been installed which conduct water from pump house to spigot-type water valves, *fuki dashi guchi*;[19] this enables farmers to manipulate water supply in each individual field. Increasingly, underdrainage networks, *chika haisui mō*, are also being constructed during field reorganization.[20] Such fine-tuning at the site level appears to affect all facets of wet-paddy or dry-field production, including water supply, distribution, and drainage; the mechanization of a formerly labor-intensive cultivation system; greater protection from natural catastrophes, both flood and drought-related; and improvement of transportation systems connecting field, village, and market.[21]

Such visual presentation of field-level changes resulting from infrastructure investment projects adds detail to this chapter's evolving definition of land improvement policy in Japan. Specifically, the comprehensive nature of this development program should be under-

---

[19] The spigot-type water valve, *fuki dashi guchi*, is a facility composed of two sets of valves that allow direct control of water at the individual field level. By opening the main valve, water flows into the field through a ball-type spigot; both the timing of water distribution and manipulation of absolute water depth can be regulated by this facility. This device is illustrated in Latz, *Nihon ni okeru kangai* [Irrigation in Japan]: 76.

[20] Underdrainage, *ankyo haisui*, is a method of subsurface drainage aimed at removal of residual surface water either on top of or within the soil of a wet-paddy field. The general designation for underdrainage facilities is underdrainage network, *chika haisui mō*. The underdrainage network is usually composed of a collecting drain, *shusui kyo*, which collects excess water from the lateral drain and guides it to the drainage canal; and a modern relief well, *haisui ben*, a facility that functions as a discharge valve by regulating the flow of excess water. For illustration, see Latz, *Nihon ni okeru kangai* [Irrigation in Japan]: 77.

[21] The comprehensive impact of land improvement projects, *tochi kairyō jigyō*, particularly in relation to individual field management, has been further described as follows: "The influence of the land improvement scheme thus affects the whole of the management of the rice producing holding, from the processes of tillage, harrowing, and leveling down to harvesting and transport, and we may say that it was the land improvement scheme which made possible the adoption of all the notable features of recent agricultural technology--the 'heat-conserving semi-inundated' nursery bed, the improvement of fertilizer application, disease and pest control, and mechanization." Tsuchiya, *Progress in Japanese Agriculture*: 209. (Explicit consideration of water control is curiously absent from this description).

scored; reorganization of agricultural areas, both by elevating the degree of water control and by rationalizing land parcels at the site level, appears to be a major goal of this policy. It is important to emphasize, however, that the illustrations, particularly figure 3, represent only a conceptualization of land improvement policy objectives. In practice, the pattern of investment varies according to regional differences in the social, economic, and environmental circumstances that shape a given area of agricultural production. It is remarkable to note, for example, that only an estimated one-third of Japan's arable land has been consolidated at the scale of 30 *āru*, the policy objective established by the Japanese Ministry of Agriculture, Forestry and Fisheries since 1963.[22] This distinction between concept and practice can be clarified by analyzing the operational, fiscal, and distributional features of post-World War II infrastructure investment projects from two perspectives: first through review of the national characteristics of land improvement projects, *tochi kairyō jigyō*; and second, through case-study analysis of a specific agricultural setting, the Kantō plain, particularly Saitama prefecture. (The latter will receive extended comment in chapter 4).

Post-World War II Characteristics of Land Improvement Projects

The main features of post-World War II land improvement projects can be discussed succinctly in terms of project type, administrative structure, and level of public subsidization. These points are summarized by chart 3 and table 1. With regard to chart 3, two trends are dominant: a decline in projects for land reclamation, *kaikon*, and in construction or refurbishing of mainline irrigation and drainage canals, *yōhaisui kansen kairyō*; and a corresponding increase in projects for farmland consolidation, *hojō seibi*, farm road consolidation, *nōdō seibi*, and comprehensive village consolidation, *nōson sōgō seibi*. Investment activity related to farmland consolidation, that is, promotion of enlarged field units in order to stimulate the diffusion of machinery, and the establishment of individual water control facilities at the field level, often including underdrainage networks, represents perhaps the most significant trend in post-World War II Japanese agricultural development.[23]

---

[22] See Nōrinsuisanshō, *Tochi kairyō no zenyō* [Comprehensive Summary of Land Improvement], 1982: 30.

[23] The data used and trends evident in chart 3 can be qualified as follows: the investment data used here are not well defined in the Japanese literature. Technically, the vertical axis represents a percentage of the total budget for *nōgyō kiban seibi* allotted to each project. However, these data do not refer to the number of completed projects, or whether or not the budget allocation is based on actual expenditures or on approximate calculations. If land improvement projects are analyzed in terms of their total number, those for farm road

Table 1 identifies the degree of government subsidization for a variety of land improvement projects.[24] A three-tiered subsidization structure is evident which specifies public financing according to type of project, size of area benefited, and level of government acting as executor. According to this subsidization system, the principal manager of a land improvement project can be one of three entities: the central government, *kokuei jigyō*; the prefectural government, *kenei jigyō*; or a site-level organization, *dantaiei jigyō*. In each case the most important administrative criterion is the size of benefited area; size, in turn, determines the principal manager and the cost-sharing formula for a given project. Government-operated projects, for example, have the largest area and, based on the Land Improvement Law of 1949, the affected prefectures are required to pay for certain development costs. The prefectures may collect all or part of these costs from the beneficiaries through local organizations. The same pattern of cost-sharing is found in both prefecture-operated and organization-operated projects, although in each case there are differences of scale, designation of principal manager, and amount of subsidization available to each participating group other than the national government, e.g., the pre-

---

consolidation, *nōdō seibi*, are most numerous, followed by protection of agricultural lands susceptible to natural disaster, *nōchi bōsai hozen*, and farmland consolidation, *hojō seibi*. In contrast, if projects are assessed in terms of their total cost, irrigation and drainage, *kangai haisui*, rank first, followed by farmland consolidation, and agricultural land development, *nōyōchi kaihatsu*. Because farmland consolidation ranks high from either perspective, and because it represents the application of civil engineering works which provide the opportunity for a greater degree of water control and mechanization of the production process, it can be identified as the most significant trend in post-World War II investment in the agricultural infrastructure. See Nōrinsuisanshō, *Tochi kairyō no zenyō* [Comprehensive Summary of Land Improvement], 1979: 290; Shibata, "Nōgyō suiri no shisutemu" [Agricultural Water-Use System]: 79-81.

[24] There are two main categories of subsidies, *hojokin*, for the Japanese agricultural sector: those that support crop or livestock production and those for land improvement programs. The total number of agricultural subsidies in both categories amounts to approximately 148. Such government-based support, either to farmers or agricultural organizations, is referred to as institutional financing, *seido kinyū*, and is administered by the Agriculture, Forestry and Fisheries Finance Corporation, *Nōrin Gyogyō Kinyū Kōko*. In the case of land improvement projects, *tochi kairyō jigyō*, this financial organ is the main source of loans for the beneficiaries' share of all associated costs, by means of financing for the nonsubsidized portion, *hojo zan yūshi*. Two points should be emphasized: (1) such monies are almost always automatically available at low interest (around 5 percent a year); and (2) these loans are not extended directly to the beneficiaries but to the Land Improvement District, *Tochi Kairyō Ku* (or another legally recognized organization), which, as the debtor, performs the task of collecting repayment from the affected parties. A separate and entirely different type of monetary support system, one that is connected to the Agricultural Cooperative Association, *Nōgyō Kyōdo Kumiai (Nōkyō)*, is Agricultural Cooperative Association financing, *kumiai kinyū*.

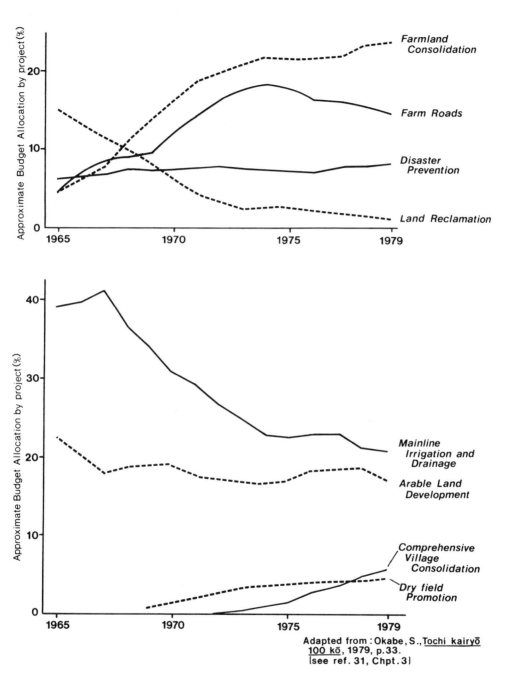

Chart 3. Projects for agricultural infrastructure consolidation, 1965-79.

Adapted from : Okabe, S., Tochi kairyō 100 kō, 1979, p.33. (see ref. 31, Chpt. 3)

Table 1. *Adoptive Standards for Projects, Subsidization Rate, and Beneficiary's Share of Project Cost and Conditions for Financing and Redemption*

Type of project	Executor	Adoption standard[1]	Share of project cost			Condition of financing and redemption of beneficiary's share	
			National	Prefecture	Local	Interest (%)	Number of years (unredeemable period)
Irrigation and drainage	National	*Benefited Area* Over 3,000 ha.	60 (58)[2]	20 (21)[2]	20 (21)[2]	5.0	17 (2)[2]
	Prefecture	Over 200 ha.	50	25	25	6.05	25 (10)[3]
	Association	Over 20 ha.	45	--	55	5.05	25 (10)[3]
Arable land development	National	*Reclaimed Area* Over 400 ha.	75 (74)[2]	12.5 (13)[2]	12.5 (13)[2]	5.0	15 (3)[2]
	Prefecture	Over 40 ha.	65	17.5	17.5	6.05	25 (10)[2,3]
	Association	Over 10 ha.	55	--	45	5.05	25 (10) [2,3]
Farmland consolidation	Prefecture	*Benefited Area* Over 200 ha. [ha.][4]	45	27.5	27.5	6.05	25 (10)[3,5]
	Association	Over 20 ha.	45	--	55	5.05	25 (10)[3,5]
Without subsidy	General case	(Irrigation, consolidation, farm road, etc.)	--	--	100	4.5	25 (10)[2,3]
	Reduction of interest		--	--	100	3.5	25 (10)[2,3]

Source: Okabe, S. *Tochi Kairyō 100 Kō* [100 Lectures on Land Improvement]: 27.

1 Main islands.
2 Special financing possible.
3 If income per beneficiary less than 3 million yen, 80 percent repayment required within specific period.
4 Site where there is more than 25 percent conversion from wet-paddy.
5 Case where 30 āru replotment is less than two-thirds.

fecture or such local organizations as the LID, municipalities, Agricultural Cooperative Associations, or independent groups of farmers. Organization-operated projects are the most numerous.[25]

The amount of public funding available for infrastructure investment is massive, amounting to $3.2 billion in 1981, approximately 2 percent of the national budget, an estimated 14 percent of the total amount of money for public works. Such public financial support for contemporary land improvement projects is subsumed under the budgetary item referred to as agricultural infrastructure consolidation, *nōgyō kiban seibi*[26], as authorized by the Agricultural Basic Law of 1961, *Nōgyō Kihon Hō*.[27] This law responds to problems found in the primary sector, particularly growing income disparities between those employed in the agricultural and industrial sectors, a consequence of rapid economic growth after World War II and the concomitant phenomenon of acute depopulation in certain rural areas, by establishing "fundamental" or "basic" goals for crop production,

---

[25] A second category of land improvement projects, in which different administrative criteria are applied, includes: independent prefecture-operated projects, *kentandoku jigyō*, often abbreviated as *kentan;* and unsubsidized projects, *hihojo jigyō*. The former is promoted under prefectural management without subsidy from the national government, while the latter receives no form of subsidy from any level of government. This second category is also referred to as a kind of land improvement project, since institutional financing, *seido kinyū*, can be utilized. Interest on money loaned is generally low, between 5 and 6 percent, and repayment usually does not begin until ten years after project completion. These observations are summarized, in part, by table 1.

[26] Utilizing 1982 national data only, it is possible to estimate the average amount of investment for *nōgyō kiban seibi*, agricultural infrastructure consolidation, per household and per hectare, for each prefecture. (Note: $1 is equal to 200 yen.) In the household case, the national average is 237,000 yen ($1,185), with Hokkaidō highest at 1,322,000 yen ($6,610), and Tokyo lowest at 20,000 yen ($100). The average national investment per hectare, on the other hand, is 199,000 yen ($995), with Shimane highest at 478,000 yen ($2,390), and Tokyo lowest at 44,000 yen ($220). See Nōrinsuisanshō, *Tochi kairyō no zenyō* [Comprehensive Summary of Land Improvement], 1982: 325; this analysis is based in part on personal correspondence with K. Shibata, Faculty of Economics, Shinshū University. Perhaps the most readily comprehensible financial figure of this kind is the estimate, as of the mid-1970s, that average infrastructure investment costs per hectare in Japan were in excess of $10,000. This figure represents the costs for field replotment, main irrigation and drainage canal facilities, terminal point irrigation and drainage facilities, and other costs associated with *tochi kairyō*, land improvement. See Takashige Kimura, "Japan--1," in *Farm Water Management for Rice Cultivation* (Tokyo: Asian Productivity Organization, 1977): 256-59. Hayami has calculated similar data for the period from the late 1940s to the early 1960s, concluding that the ratio of government to private investment was consistently high; as of 1962 the government percentage equaled nearly 69 percent. The total amount of land affected between 1950 and 1965 was estimated to be approximately 2.2 million hectares. See Hayami, *Century of Agricultural Growth:* 172, 178, 235.

[27] See Nōrinsuisanshō, ed., *Tochi kairyō yōran* [Summary of Land Improvement]: 110-13.

distribution of farm commodities, and the general structure of Japanese agriculture. The specific objectives for crop production are three-fold: (1) diversification of agricultural activity, i.e., the encouragement of crop or livestock production in addition to wet-paddy, leading to (2) stabilization of the economic base of individual farm households through higher incomes, together with (3) introduction of modern cropping methods that rely on comprehensive agricultural mechanization. The goal with regard to farm commodity distribution focuses attention on the need to upgrade the transport network in rural areas. Finally, goals for the agricultural structure include identification of the need to develop a comprehensive program of government-based economic support for agricultural development through such subsidy programs as agricultural structure improvement projects, *nōgyō kōzō kaizen jigyō*, and by means of other investment.[28]

The contemporary national pattern of land improvement activity is shown in map 2, which portrays both the distribution and density of a total of 9,147 LIDs, as of March 31, 1981.[29] This figure represents a decline of 30 percent from a post-World War II high of 13,146 LIDs, in 1961. Approximately 68.9 percent of the 1981 total are concerned primarily with water control in wet-paddy areas, specifically irrigation and drainage canal maintenance, *iji kanri*.[30] Initially, in the first decade after the legislation

---

[28] There is a great deal of confusion in the Japanese literature regarding financing for investment in the agricultural infrastructure. All projects that attempt to alter the condition or structure of agricultural production by improving labor productivity, rationalizing agricultural water use, and encouraging diversification of crop production are called agricultural structure improvement projects, *nōgyō kōzō kaizen jigyō*. A related term is agricultural infrastructure consolidation, *nōgyō kiban seibi*, which is often used interchangeably with the program for agricultural structure improvement. Precisely speaking, these two terms should not be used synonymously; agricultural infrastructure consolidation refers to the budgetary item that acts as a subsidy for agricultural structure improvement projects. This distinction may be clarified further by noting that agricultural structure improvement is the policy goal, whereas agricultural infrastructure consolidation is the financial vehicle for its realization. The agenda for agricultural structure improvement projects was established generally by the Agricultural Basic Law, *Nōgyō Kihon Hō*, enacted in 1961. Projects aim specifically at the introduction of machinery in farming operations and the modernization of agricultural management; consolidation of landholdings is a major objective. The goal of farmland consolidation was reinforced further in 1963 with enactment of a governmental subsidization scheme which aimed at establishing farm parcels 30 *āru* (30 x 100 meters) in size, referred to as *hojō seibi jigyō*, farmland consolidation projects.

[29] Survey results were catalogued initially by Shibata Kyōhei, Faculty of Economics, Shinshū University. Additional discussion of LID distribution can be found in Nishikawa, "Nihon ni okeru tochi kairyō ku no bumpu" [Distribution of LIDs in Japan]: 17-24.

[30] Personal correspondence, Shibata Kyōhei, Faculty of Economics, Shinshū University. See also Shibata, "Saitama ken minumadai yōsui ni okeru nōgyō suiri shisutemu" [Agricultural Water-Use System in Minumadai Canal of Saitama Prefecture].

was promulgated in 1949, nearly all LIDs aimed at resolution of water-control problems; however, as noted in chart 3, there has been a steady increase since the 1960s in farmland consolidation, farm road development, and other projects that either combine water control facilities with arable land reorganization, or are concerned exclusively with infrastructure investment unrelated to the water distribution and drainage network. A majority of present-day LIDs are smaller than 100 hectares in size, and a mere 7 percent are larger than 1,000 hectares; in the post-World War II period, at the national level, there has been a steady decrease in those smaller than 50 hectares, and a corresponding increase in those over 1,000 hectares, with the latter doubling their share of the total number between 1950 and 1981.[31]

Map 2 is based specifically on review of the register of district names, *meibo*, in each prefecture. The registers contain information on the number of members, area benefited, project outline, date of establishment, official name, etc. Four observations can be made in the case of the map at hand. (1) Districts are numerous in: the four prefectures of the Tone watershed (Tochigi, Ibaraki, Chiba, and Saitama); central Japan, adjacent to the Sea of Japan (Fukui and Ishikawa); areas with a high ratio of irrigation pond/reservoirs, *tameike*, to arable land (Hyōgo); and southern Kyūshū (Kagoshima). (2) Districts are not numerous in highly urbanized parts of Japan (Tokyo, Kanagawa, Ōsaka, Kyōto). (3) There are significant differences in the amounts of arable land in the four regions with large numbers of districts: Kagoshima prefecture to the south, as well as the four Tone water-shed prefectures, located in the largest of Japan's alluvial plains, the Kantō, have relatively more farmland, averaging over 100,000 hectares each, and may be contrasted to the two prefectures in central Japan, which have considerably less, averaging 50,000 hectares each, with the irrigation pond/reservoir case residing in the middle at slightly less than 100,000 hectares. (4) It can be inferred from this superficial geographical analysis that the regional variation in the number of LIDs cannot be explained in terms of the total amount of arable land per prefecture; other environmental, as well as socioeconomic factors need to be considered.[32] These observations will be discussed further in chapter 4 with reference to the Kanto plain as one

---

[31] Nōrinsuisanshō Kōzōkaizenkyoku Kensetsubu, ed., *Tochi kairyō no zenyō* [Comprehensive Summary of Land Improvement], 1979: 348; updated with 1981 data by Shibata, "Nōgyō suiri shisutemu" [The Agricultural Water-Use System]: 81.

[32] The four-point interpretation presented here is derived from lectures by Shibata Kyōhei, University of Tokyo, 1982. An important qualification is that although Kagoshima prefecture is combined with the Kantō prefectures for classification purposes, only one-third of its arable land is devoted to wet-paddy fields, *suiden*, with the remainder committed to dry-field agriculture, *hatake nōgyō*.

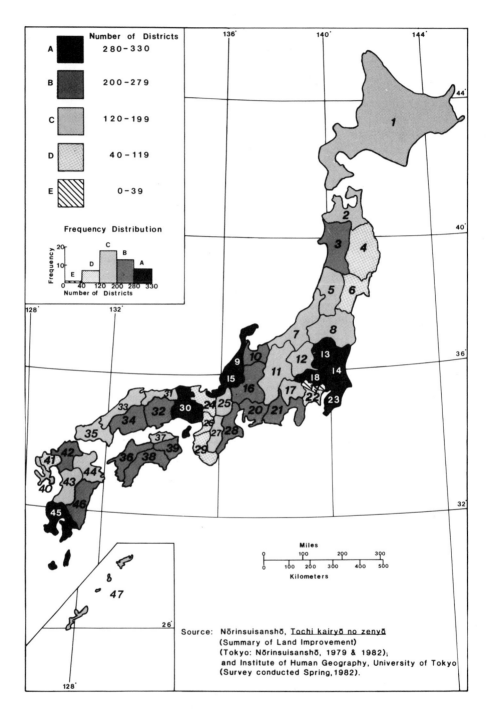

Map 2. *The national distribution of Land Improvement Districts, 1981.*

region with a remarkably high concentration of LIDs; Saitama prefecture will be investigated in particular detail.

Over the course of the twentieth century a distinct policy has emerged for government-supported investment in the Japanese agricultural infrastructure. This investment program has been shaped primarily by two pieces of legislation promulgated fifty years apart, the Arable Land Reorganization Law of 1899 and the Land Improvement Law of 1949. A summary comparison of their similarities and differences serves to clarify the characteristics of each and their combined significance to the study of agricultural development in Japan. Two observations may be made regarding complementary features of these policies: each may be said to promote reorganization of agricultural areas through direct infrastructure investment;[33] and in addition, each relies on a legally established administrative unit that is responsible for borrowing monies from governmental or pseudo-governmental sources, for assuming beneficiary debt, and for exercising limited coercive powers to guarantee farmer participation in a given project. Significant differences between these two policies should also be noted: participant qualifications have changed since the post-World War II land reform, *nōchi kaikaku*, granting membership to both tenants and landowners; the amount of money available to subsidize infrastructure development has increased dramatically in the post-World War II period; and there has been a streamlining of administrative unit function at the site level, resulting in the combination of maintenance and development responsibilities within the LID. The first half century of this legislation was

---

[33] Paradoxically, the terminology used in the pre-World War II legislation implies reorganization, but in practice the policy aimed primarily at renovation and development of irrigation and drainage facilities.

Key to map 2

1	Hokkaidō	13	Tochigi	25	Shiga	37	Kagawa
2	Aomori	14	Ibaraki	26	Ōsaka	38	Kōchi
3	Akita	15	Fukui	27	Nara	39	Tokushima
4	Iwate	16	Gifu	28	Mie	40	Nagasaki
5	Yamagata	17	Yamanashi	29	Wakayama	41	Saga
6	Miyagi	18	Saitama	30	Hyōgo	42	Fukuoka
7	Niigata	19	Tokyo	31	Tottori	43	Kumamoto
8	Fukushima	20	Aichi	32	Okayama	44	Ōita
9	Ishikawa	21	Shizuoka	33	Shimane	45	Kagoshima
10	Toyama	22	Kanagawa	34	Hiroshima	46	Miyazaki
11	Nagano	23	Chiba	35	Yamaguchi	47	Okinawa
12	Gunma	24	Kyōto	36	Ehime		

characterized by investment projects that aimed primarily at mainline irrigation network development. Since 1961, however, there has been an increase in the number of farmland consolidation projects, often including underdrainage, as well as projects for farm road development.

There is a tendency in the Japanese literature to use the designation *tochi kairyō*, land improvement, to describe all twentieth-century examples of investment in the agricultural infrastructure. Legally speaking, however, the meaning of the term can refer only to those projects authorized by the 1949 legislation. This distinction between pre- and postwar policies is important in two respects. While land improvement legislation can be seen as a continuation of infrastructure investment programs initiated earlier in the century, it is now characterized by a much wider range of projects which seek to promote the coordinated development of land and water resources in the primary sector. In addition, these projects not only allow for the application of increasingly sophisticated civil engineering technology, but represent significant changes in the legal, social, and financial relationship between farmers and government in the post-World War II period. The latter observation is perhaps best illustrated by the main functions of the LID, an organization with administrative responsibilities for financing, construction, and maintenance of field-level facilities which support agricultural production.

Chapter 4 will further explore the functions of the LID, particularly as an administrative unit for investment in and maintenance of the agricultural infrastructure. The Kantō plain and Saitama prefecture will serve as the object of such analysis based on examination of the distributional pattern of land improvement activity in the post-World War II period. That nationwide, land improvement projects for farmland consolidation, *hojō seibi jigyō*, have benefited only an estimated one-third of the arable land in the agricultural sector suggests that there exists an apparent discrepancy between proposals and actual practices at the site level. Recognition of this discrepancy between policy objectives and policy accomplishments will guide the Saitama case study; the central question will be whether or not the prefecture displays a comprehensive approach to development and rationalization of land and water use in its primary sector. The implications of such case-study review to overall evaluation of the strengths and weaknesses of this particular policy for agricultural infrastructure development will be considered in the concluding portions of chapter 4 and in chapter 5.

Chapter 4

THE CASE OF SAITAMA PREFECTURE AND THE
MINUMA LAND IMPROVEMENT DISTRICT

This chapter will discuss in the context of a particular agricultural setting in Japan the operational characteristics of the post-World War II *Tochi Kairyō Ku*, Land Improvement District (LID).[1] The site selected for in-depth analysis is Saitama prefecture, in the heart of Japan's largest alluvial plain, the Kantō. The reasons for selecting Saitama are two-fold: its location in a region of Japan with a high level of investment activity (see map 2); and the assumption that proximity to the Tokyo metropolis defines a clear-cut set of contemporary social and economic pressures typically found in many of Japan's traditional agricultural areas. Discussion of land improvement programs in Saitama will focus upon the prefectural and site levels. In the case of the latter, attention will be directed to the Minuma LID, the administrative unit with maintenance responsibility for the Minumadai irrigation canal. Maps 3, 4 and 5 provide cartographic presentation of the research site, in terms of the Kantō plain, Saitama prefecture, and Minumadai canal irrigation area.[2]

The framework for the discussion to follow has been established by the interlocking themes examined in chapters 1, 2, and 3. They are: the language of Japanese agriculture, the socioeconomic and environmental features of agricultural development in the twentieth century, and the evolution of policy for land improvement, particularly in the post-World

---

[1]   The appellation *Tochi Kairyō Ku*, Land Improvement District, will be abbreviated in this chapter as LID.

[2]   Thematic presentation of Saitama prefecture and the Minumadai beneficiary area is presented in maps 6 through 9.

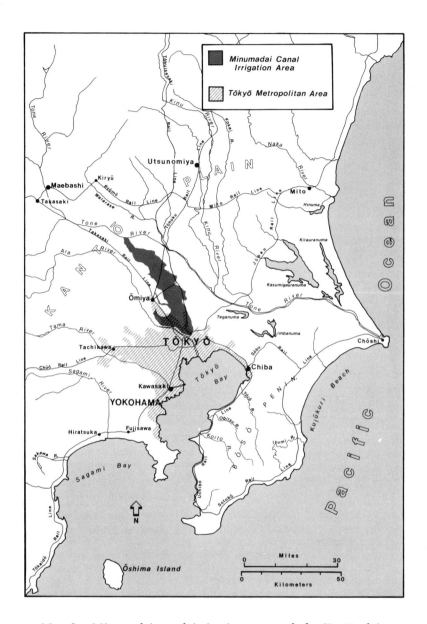

Map 3. Minumadai canal irrigation area and the Kantō plain.
Sources: Minuma Tochi Kairyō Ku, "Minuma tochi kairyō ku iji kanri keikakusho fuzu" [Plan-
ning Documents and Illustrations for Maintenance Control in the Minuma LID]; Shibata, "Daitoshi kinkō ni okeru nōgyō suiri soshiki no henyō" [Evolution and Response of Agricultural
Water Use Organizations to Suburbanization and Demand for Water Rationalization]: map 1,
p. 7; and (with reference to Tokyo metropolitan area), Kensetsushō, Kokudochiribu, ed., *Nihon
kokusei chizuchō* [National Atlas of Japan]: 75.

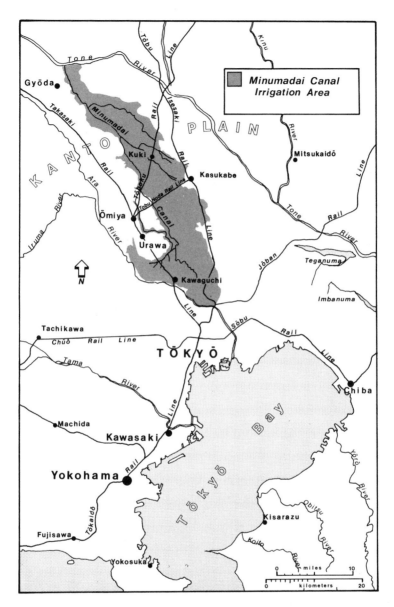

Map 4. *Minumadai canal irrigation area and Tokyo Bay.*
Sources: Minuma Tochi Kairyō Ku, "Minuma tochi kairyō ku iji kanri keikakusho fuzu"
[Planning Documents and Illustrations for Maintenance Control in the Minuma LID]; Shibata,
"Daitoshi kinkō ni okeru nōgyō suiri soshiki no henyō" [Evolution and Response of Agricultural
Water Use Organizations to Suburbanization and Demand for Water Rationalization]: map 1,
p. 7; and (with reference to Tokyo metropolitan area), Kensetsushō, Kokudochiribu, ed., *Nihon
kokusei chizuchō* [National Atlas of Japan]: 75.

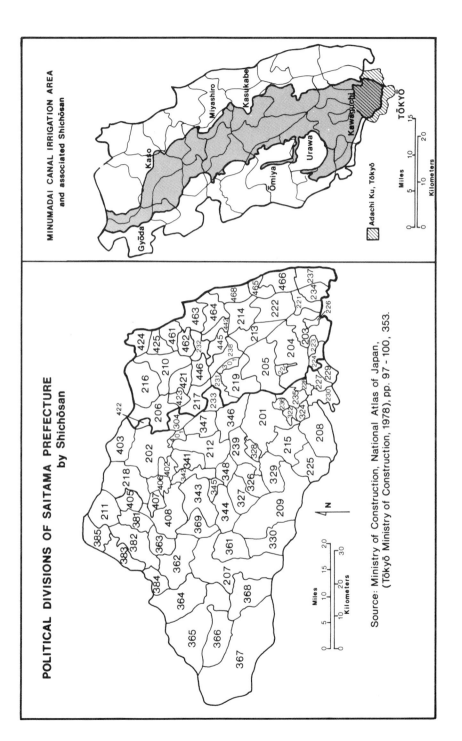

Map 5. Political divisions of Saitama prefecture.

War II period. The relationship between these themes is to be clarified further in this chapter through investigation of the ways in which land improvement policy is shaped by site conditions, both environmental and socioeconomic, resulting in a distinct pattern of infrastructure investment. This point can be restated in conceptual and practical terms. In concept, the purpose of land improvement policy in the postwar period is to promote coordinated development of the agricultural infrastructure for crop production in Japan's primary sector. In practice, however, site conditions can be expected to modify such policy goals, an adjustment process that is reflected by the distribution and types of land improvement projects and activities found in a given agricultural area.

The primary goal of this chapter is to focus on the ways in which policy is adjusted to conditions at the site level in Saitama prefecture. This will be addressed through the analysis of LIDs in Saitama as to whether or not this prefecture displays a comprehensive approach to development and rationalization of land and water use. Two questions guide the investigation: what is the respective pattern of investment in projects related to the agricultural infrastructure, particularly for land readjustment, *kukaku seiri*, and farmland consolidation, *hojō seibi*; and what is the pattern of investment for water control facilities, as reflected by the activity of maintenance of irrigation and drainage canals, *iji kanri*, and projects for agricultural water-use rationalization, *nōgyō yōsui gōrika*? Serious doubts can be raised about the extent to which the wide-ranging activities of LIDs reflect a coordinated approach to agricultural development in Saitama. Such analysis should also clarify the definition of land improvement policy presented heretofore by identifying how this particular program for agricultural development in Japan has attempted to promote a goal of increasing agricultural production without disrupting the traditional pattern of agricultural water use. Overall assessment of land improvement programs in Japan, based on the case-study findings, will take place in the conclusion to this chapter and in chapter 5.[3]

---

[3] The pages to follow are based on a year-long course the author participated in, from 1982 through 1983, entitled, *Jinbun Chiri Gaku Yagai Jisshū* [Preparatory Seminar for Field Work on Japanese Agricultural Water Use], Institute of Human Geography, University of Tokyo, Shibata Kyōhei, instructor. Research growing out of this seminar includes: Shibata, "Daitoshi kinkō ni okeru nōgyō suiri soshiki no henyō" [Evolution and Response of Agricultural Water-Use Organizations to Suburbanization and Demand for Water Rationalization]; Shibata, "Saitama ken minumadai yōsui ni okeru nōgyō suiri shisutemu" [Agricultural Water-Use System in Minumadai Canal of Saitama Prefecture]; and Latz, *Nihon ni okeru kangai* [Irrigation in Japan]. A revised version of chapter 4 is Latz, "Agricultural Development: The Case of Saitama Prefecture."

Land Improvement and the Kantō Plain

National data on infrastructure investment in Japan indicate that the Kantō plain,[4] composed of Tochigi, Ibaraki, Gunma, Saitama, Chiba, Tokyo, and Kanagawa prefectures, is distinguished by a large number of LIDs (see map 2). As of March 31, 1981, 16.1 percent, or 1,472, of the nation's 9,147 LIDs were located in the Kantō region, with administrative responsibilities for infrastructure investment and maintenance on two-thirds of the arable land, totaling approximately 613,500 hectares.[5] Of the existing LIDs, 78.9 percent are concerned primarily with *iji kanri*, irrigation and drainage canal maintenance, considerably higher than the nationwide average of 68.9 percent.[6] Other salient points regarding agricultural activity on the Kantō plain are that it is the location of 14.3 percent of Japan's arable land, 15.4 percent of the total number of agricultural households, and 8.7 percent of all

---

[4] Definition of the Kantō region differs according to statistical source in the Japanese literature. The Nōrinsuisanshō's most comprehensive definition includes ten prefectures: the five interior prefectures of Ibaraki, Tochigi, Gunma, Yamanashi, and Nagano; and the four coastal prefectures of Saitama, Chiba, Tokyo, and Kanagawa (Shizuoka is sometimes added). The definition used in this paper refers to the Kantō alluvial plain, excluding consideration of Nagano, Yamanashi, and Shizuoka. Compare: Nōrinsuisanshō Tōkei Jōhōbu, *Dai 57ji nōrinsuisanshō tōkeihyō* [The 57th Statistical Yearbook of the Ministry of Agriculture, Forestry and Fisheries] (Tokyo: Nōrinsuisanshō Tōkei Jōhōbu, 1982), introduction pp. 24-26, text p. 5; and Nōrinsuisanshō, *Tochi kairyō no zenyō* [Comprehensive Summary of Land Improvement], 1982: 325, 353.

[5] As noted in chapter 3, the standard government reference for information on policy for land improvement projects, *tochi kairyō jigyō*, and the Land Improvement District, *Tochi Kairyō Ku*, is Nōrinsuisanshō, *Tochi kairyō no zenyō* [Comprehensive Summary of Land Improvement], 1982. Specific reference to distribution, membership, and size can be found on pp. 372 and 376-77. See also Nōrinsuisanshō, *Tochi kairyō no zenyō* [Comprehensive Summary of Land Improvement], 1979: 340. Government statistics were also evaluated through a national survey of registers of LID names, *meibo*, by prefecture, conducted in the spring of 1982, by the Institute of Human Geography, University of Tokyo, as administered by Nishikawa Osamu and Shibata Kyōhei. Cartographic presentation of survey results can be found in map 2, above.

[6] These percentages are based on review of the registers of LID names, *meibo*, for the Kantō region, as part of a survey conducted in the spring of 1982 and calculated by Shibata Kyōhei; data used in this case include evaluation of LID function as of April 1, 1982. Further discussion may be found in Shibata, "Saitama ken minumadai yōsui ni okeru nōgyō suiri shisutemu" [Agricultural Water-Use System in Minumadai Canal of Saitama Prefecture]: tables 1 and 4. LIDs for *iji kanri*, irrigation and drainage canal maintenance, may be defined as organizations with responsibility for annual levy collection from each farmer benefiting from water distribution. The money is used to sustain the operation of the irrigation network. This type of LID may be distinguished from LIDs for *kukaku seiri*, land readjustment, or *hojō seibi*, farmland consolidation, which are not concerned with maintenance of or investment in facilities related to the irrigation and drainage network.

investment for *nōgyō kiban seibi*, agricultural infrastructure consolidation.[7] A comparison of farm households and arable land indicates that land-holdings average 1.08 hectares, somewhat below the national mean of 1.19 hectares.[8] This point should be underscored, along with the fact that the amount of *nōgyō kiban seibi* investment is low in comparison with the relatively high number of LIDs, suggesting that land improvement activity is at present dormant in large parts of the Kantō. This situation may be attributed to extraordinarily high urban pressures to convert farmland to residential, commercial, or industrial uses; the Keihin metropolitan area is estimated to have contained 28.4 million people in 1980, approximately one-quarter of the national population.[9]

The concentration of agricultural land, a relatively large number of LIDs, and urbanization pressures combine to make the Kantō plain a unique region in the Japanese archipelago, and especially suitable for in-depth analysis of the state of contemporary agriculture. Of the seven prefectures that comprise the region, Saitama may be identified as a representative agricultural setting in three respects. First, it contains a large number of LIDs, 287, ranking seventh in the nation and fourth in Kantō after Ibaraki (331), Tochigi (321), and Chiba (296).[10] Second, land improvement activity in Saitama is distinguished by the degree to which accumulated hectarage benefiting from infrastructure investment exceeds the total amount of arable land in the prefecture, by roughly 22 percent, ranking it fourth in the nation, and highest in Kantō.[11] Third, Saitama boasts a large number of

---

[7] These calculations are based on the following sources: Nōrinsuisanshō, *Tochi kairyō no zenyō* [Comprehensive Summary of Land Improvement], 1982: 325; and Nōrinsuisanshō, *Poketto nōrin suisan tōkei, 1983* [Agriculture, Forestry and Fishery Statistics, 1983 Pocket Edition]: 108, 124. It should be emphasized that these statistics represent data for only one year and do not necessarily reflect trends over time.

[8] Nōrinsuisanshō, *Poketto nōrin suisan tōkei, 1983* [Agriculture, Forestry and Fishery Statistics, 1983 Pocket Edition]: 108, 124.

[9] Chauncy D. Harris, "The Urban and Industrial Transformation of Japan," *Geographical Review* 72, no. 1 (January 1982): 83-84. The Keihin major metropolitan area refers to the commuting zone surrounding the cities of Tokyo, Yokohama, and Kawasaki, as recognized in each population census since 1960. The Tokyo metropolitan area, as defined by the Kensetsushō, *Nihon kokusei chizuchō* [National Atlas of Japan]: 75, is shown on map 3. (The Tokyo area, composed of Tokyo, Kanagawa, Chiba, Saitama, and Ibaraki prefectures, had a net population in-migration of 7.7 million between 1950 and 1980). See Harris, "Urban Transformation of Japan": 70. For specific population data on Saitama prefecture, see map 8.

[10] The LID totals used here are based on Nōrinsuisanshō, *Tochi kairyō no zenyō* [Comprehensive Summary of Land Improvement], 1982: 376.

[11] The high proportion of accumulated hectarage or overlap, 139,811 hectares, as contrasted to the Saitama arable land total of 109,400 hectares (source: see note 6), will be discussed

LIDs despite its proximity to Tokyo or the fact that it is a prefecture that is estimated to have experienced net population in-migration of 1.9 million people between 1950 and 1980, averaging 63,000 people per year from 1950 to 1975, and 70,000 people per year from 1976 to 1980.[12] The main features of LID activity in Saitama, particularly in terms of magnitude, distribution, changing function, and degree of arable land overlap, will be investigated below.

Land Improvement in Saitama

Between 1950 and 1981, a total of 612 LIDs were established in Saitama prefecture.[13] Of these, 325 were either dissolved or amalgamated, so that the 1982 number of active LIDs equaled 287.[14] The pattern of establishment follows an L-shaped curve, with the largest number, 121, originating in 1952.[15] The vast majority of LIDs formed at this time had actually func-

---

below. As used here the term indicates the intensity of arable land investment, that is, the total number of hectares under the jurisdiction of LIDs in Saitama prefecture. An analogy to conventional analysis of agricultural land use would be reference to the multiple cropping index or rate of arable land utilization in a given area, although, in the case at hand, it is not the number of crops produced per year but level of infrastructure investment that is identified.

[12] Harris, "Urban Transformation of Japan": 69-70. See also map 8.

[13] This calculation is based on the following sources: Saitama Ken Tochi Kairyō Jigyō Dantai Rengō Kai, ed., *Saitama no tochi kairyō* [Land Improvement in Saitama] (Urawa: Saitama Ken, 1977): 612-55; Nōrinsuisanshō, *Tochi kairyō no zenyō* [Comprehensive Summary of Land Improvement], 1979: 340; Nōrinsuisanshō, *Tochi kairyō no zenyō* [Comprehensive Summary of Land Improvement], 1982: 372; and Saitama Ken Nōrinbu Kōchikeikakuka, *Showa 57 shigatsu tsuitachi genzai tochi kairyō ku meibo* [April 1, 1982, Register of Land Improvement Districts] (Urawa: Saitama Ken, 1982).

[14] The fact that dissolved or amalgamated LIDs (325) outnumber existing LIDs (287) is a reflection of the development objective, and the fiscal circumstances, of a given land improvement project. LIDs normally dissolve upon repayment of borrowed monies from the *Nōrin Gyogyō Kinyū Kōko*, Agriculture, Forestry and Fisheries Finance Corporation, unless they assume responsibility for facilities related to *iji kanri*, irrigation and drainage canal maintenance. The distinction between existing, dissolved, and amalgamated LIDs will be discussed further below. See also table 1.

[15] It is remarkable that a total of 130 LIDs were established in Saitama prefecture by the end of 1952, representing one out of five, or 21.2 percent, of the 612 LIDs known to have existed between 1950 and 1982. Of these 130 LIDs, 108 can be traced back to pre-World War II *Futsū Suiri Kumiai*, Regular Water-Use Associations. These 108 LIDs became *iji kanri* LIDs as stipulated by the Land Improvement Law of 1949. The ebb and flow of this particular type of LID is indicated by the number that survived until 1977, totaling 76, or 70.4 percent. Of the 32 that are no longer functioning, 16 were amalgamated into other *iji kanri* LIDs, with the balance ceasing their activities altogether, probably owing to conversion of agricultural land to urban use. As of 1982, 144 LIDs or 50.2 percent of the total could be identified as *iji kanri* LIDs in Saitama prefecture. This percentage is much lower than the average for the Kantō

tioned formerly as *Fūtsu Suiri Kumiai,* Regular Water-Use Associations, organizations that were supplanted by LIDs as stipulated by the Land Improvement Law of 1949. Subsequent to 1949, the number of active LIDs grew gradually to a peak of 372, in 1968, after which they declined to the present-day total. The rate and progression of LID establishment is clearly divisible into two parts:[16] rapid initial growth representing the extension, albeit modified, of the pre-World War II organizational structure for agricultural production, with a heavy emphasis on *iji kanri,* irrigation and drainage canal maintenance; and a second stage, after 1952, representing a gradual increase in the total number of LIDs with objectives more closely related to the postwar legislation for land improvement, including projects for *kukaku seiri,* land readjustment; *hojō seibi,* farmland consolidation;[17] and, most recently, the promotion of *nōgyō yōsui gōrika,* agricultural water-use rationalization, the latter occurring primarily in urbanizing areas.[18] Specific to the goals more recently adopted were those policy decisions of the early 1960s which led to the promulgation of the *Nōgyō Kihon Hō,* Agricultural Basic Law of 1961, the *Mizu Shigen Kaihatsu Sokushin Hō,*

---

plain, which stood at 78.9 percent as of 1981. The sources for these statistics can be found in notes 5 and 13.

[16] The division of LID establishment into two stages, based on frequency, may be overly simplistic since it fails to consider changes in land improvement policy, or promulgation of new legislation, over the course of the postwar period.

[17] The argument to follow hinges on the distinctions between, and meaning of, *hojō seibi* and *kukaku seiri* expressed in chapter 3, note 4.

[18] Agricultural water-use rationalization projects, *nōgyō yōsui gōrika jigyō,* were initiated in 1974 by the Ministry of Agriculture, Forestry and Fisheries and aim at utilizing engineering techniques for improving the efficiency of water conveyance throughout the irrigation network. The objectives of such projects are two-fold: new construction or improvement of irrigation and drainage facilities whose benefited area exceeds 200 hectares; and reduction of the absolute water intake volume by more than 10 percent or, in the case where water flow is measured at a given point, reduction of the amount of water by more than 0.5 m^3/sec. Such water-use rationalization is administered by means of prefecture-operated projects only. The following points should be emphasized: (1) in the Japanese case, rationalization does not refer to alteration of the *kankō suiri ken,* customary water rights, of farmers, but relies instead on more sophisticated technology to raise the efficiency of water transfer (in effect, to capture that water lost through canal leakage); (2) the conditions prompting such projects are found primarily in rapidly suburbanizing areas where the problem of water supply and demand becomes acute (although even in such regions agricultural customary water rights have not necessarily been altered); (3) those who demand additional water, such as industrial water users, usually bear the cost of such rationalization projects in lieu of the local farmers; and (4) such rationalization is in some cases promoted by the *Mizu Shigen Kaihatsu Kōdan,* Water Resources Development Public Corporation, though at a larger scale and, proportionally, with a much greater share of investment from the national government than is true in the above mentioned prefecture-operated projects.

Water Resources Development Promotion Law of 1961, and the *Kasen Hō*, River Law of 1964.[19] These three pieces of legislation have influenced the development of projects for land improvement by setting standards for reorganization of crop-producing areas, particularly rationalization of agricultural land and water use at both the field level and at the irrigation and drainage network level.[20]

The two stages of land improvement activity in Saitama can be analyzed further as periods in which there is a distinct change in the distribution and function of infrastructure investment projects found in this prefecture. Representative LIDs with responsibility for development of the land infrastructure, as well as maintenance and renovation of a given irrigation network, will be scrutinized. In the case of the former, the presentation will concentrate on projects for *kukaku seiri*, land readjustment, and *hojō seibi*, farmland consolidation.[21] In the case of the

---

[19] These legislative acts sometimes display contradictory objectives, i.e., the *Kasen Ho* calls for coordinated river management by identifying national and prefectural rivers, yet grants legal status to the farmer's *kankō suiri ken*, customary water rights; the latter acts as an impediment to *nōgyō yōsui gōrika*, agricultural water-use rationalization, a point to be examined below. More detailed description of the *Nōgyō Kihon Hō*, Agricultural Basic Law, *Mizu Shigen Kaihatsu Sokushin Hō*, Water Resource Development Promotion Law, and the *Kasen Hō*, River Law, can be found in Latz, *Nihon ni okeru kangai* [Irrigation in Japan]: 34-36.

[20] Of these three legislative acts, the *Nōgyō Kihon Hō*, Agricultural Basic Law, has received the greatest amount of attention in the English literature. This is due to the fact that a central objective of this legislation is to promote both the diversification and the mechanization of Japanese agricultural production. The fact that the agricultural infrastructure must first be reshaped to accommodate field machinery is often lost in this discussion, hence the emphasis here on *tochi kairyō jigyō*, land improvement projects, which aim to reorganize agricultural production sites.

[21] The primary cartographic reference for this discussion will be map 6. The Saitama source (see map legend) identifies all *kukaku seiri* agricultural development projects in the prefecture between 1900 (Meiji 36) and 1981 (Showa 56); the present paper isolates for detailed analysis the period from 1949 to 1981, commencing with promulgation of the *Tochi Kairyō Hō*, Land Improvement Law. The source data are presented in both tabular and mapped form, the latter at a scale of 1:75,000. The tabular data are of particular interest, and record the following information: map reference number; site location; *shichōson*, settlement; name of responsible LID; name of LID elected head; dates of execution; administrative funding category; project area, including total *hatake*, dry-field, and *suiden*, wet-field, hectarage; scale of replotment, in *āru* (.01 hectares) and geometric dimensions; and date of dissolution, or other remarks, as applicable. The final three pages of these tables present a summary of: (1) the total number of hectares in the prefecture receiving investment, by zone, divided according to *hatake* and *suiden* designations; (2) the twenty-three types of administrative categories for investment, again with the total number of hectares affected, divided according to *suiden* and *hatake*; and (3) zonal division in terms of project replotment scale, according to total hectarage, and the *suiden/hatake* distinction. The entire period, 1900-1981, may be summarized as one in which 76,116.9 hectares of arable land received investment; 64 percent of the land affected was for *suiden* development, and only 20 percent resulted in land replotment at a scale of 30 *āru*, or larger. In the case of the latter percentage,

latter, the presentation will combine field-level information with analysis of a LID with responsibility for *iji kanri*, irrigation and drainage canal maintenance, and for *nōgyō yōsui gōrika*, agricultural water-use rationalization, in a particular water distribution network, the Minumadai irrigation canal.[22]

Pattern of Farmland Reorganization in Saitama

A total of 403 projects for *kukaku seiri*, land readjustment, covering 37,655 hectares of land, were carried out in Saitama prefecture from 1949 to 1981. The distribution and magnitude of the investment program,[23] in

---

the amount of larger-scale replotment was divided approximately equally between *suiden* and *hatake* land development. Three additional comments are in order here. First, the raw data are not totaled in terms of the number of projects per *shichōson*, settlements, in Saitama prefecture; for more effective cartographic presentation, the author has reorganized the information in terms of these ninety-two political units, utilizing census base maps, as noted above. Second, there are other analyses of the distribution of this investment data, specifically the area of Saitama prefecture associated with the Minumadai canal irrigation area: for the period 1949-81, see Gil Latz, "Kukaku seiri-type Land Improvement Trends in the Minuma LID," unpublished lecture, Graduate Student Seminar, Institute of Human Geography, University of Tokyo, November, 1983; and for the period 1900-1981, see Shibata, "Saitama ken minumadai yōsui ni okeru nōgyō suiri shisutemu" [Agricultural Water-Use System in Minumadai Canal of Saitama Prefecture], map 4. And third, there is some confusion regarding the English translation of the official title of this government publication; *nōchi seibi*, agricultural land consolidation, is used to introduce the title, followed by *kukaku seiri*, land readjustment, in parentheses. There is no meaningful English translation for the term *nōchi seibi*, and it should be viewed as a typical example of the proliferation of administrative/bureaucratic jargon in the post-World War II period. This point will be discussed further in chapter 5.

22   The primary cartographic references for this discussion will be maps 7, 8, and 9.

23   Estimates of the degree of investment and costs associated with agricultural infrastructure projects are available at both the national and prefectural levels. See: Nōrinsuisanshō, *Tochi kairyō no zenyō* [Comprehensive Summary of Land Improvement], 1982: 325; and Saitama Ken, *Saitama ken no tochi kairyō (jigyō gaiyō)* [Land Improvement in Saitama Prefecture (Project Summary)] (Urawa: Saitama Ken, 1983): 47. The categories of financial classification differ in each case, with the national level data indicating that in 1982, Saitama prefecture invested nearly 9 billion yen (an estimated $45 million [at 200 yen equal to $1]) in *nōgyō kiban seibi*, agricultural infrastructure consolidation, while the prefectural data reports that nearly 15 billion yen ($75 million) was invested in projects related to *tochi kairyō*, land improvement; the latter figure is larger because it represents monies from both national and prefectural sources. Comparison of 1982 prefectural level and national data indicates that the amount of *nōgyō kiban seibi* investment, per household (74,000 yen) and per hectare (82,000 yen) is below average in Saitama. It should be emphasized that these statistics represent data for only one year and do not necessarily represent trends over time. Additional investigation of the Saitama case, in terms of the Minumadai canal beneficiary area, was conducted in 1982-83 by students at the University of Tokyo. LIDs for *kukaku seiri*, land readjustment, and *hojō seibi*, farmland consolidation, were discovered on average to be smallest in size and highest in cost, based on thirty-three

terms of Saitama prefecture's present-day settlement pattern, *shichōson*,[24] is presented in map 6. The main zones of LID activity include Urawa-/ Omiya-/Kawagoe-*shi* (#204, 205, 201), to the south, and Gyōda-*shi*/ Kawasato-/Kisai-*machi* (#206, 423, 421), to the north; other sites with high investment, also to the north and extending in an arc from east to west, include Miyashiro-/Satte-*machi* (#442, 463), Yoshimi-*machi* (#347), and Fukaya-*shi* (#218).[25] This distributional pattern of infrastructure investment is distinct in three respects: first, two main zones of activity can be identified, one centering on Urawa (#204) to the south, and the other on Gyōda (#206) to the north, coinciding in each case with alluvial soils and relatively level parts of the prefecture; second, the areal concentration of projects is decidedly higher to the south, but the total number of LIDs is larger and more dispersed to the north, where seven *shichōson* can be identified as places with a high degree of LID activity, equal to 70 percent of the prefecture total; and third, there is almost no investment in the extreme southern and southwestern one-third of the prefecture, owing, respectively, to extensive urbanization or mountainous conditions.

The distributional pattern of investment found in map 6 can be discussed further by dividing the period under study into five-year blocks of time. Two peak periods of investment can be discerned, 1955 through 1959 and 1965 through 1969, affecting roughly 9,000 hectares in each case, or 49.4 percent of the total amount of farmland receiving infrastructure investment from 1949 to 1981.[26] Comparison of project initiation date to

---

responses to a detailed questionnaire sent to seventy-four LIDs associated with the Minuma LID beneficiary area; annual levies per farmer were as high as 10,000 yen ($50) per *tan* (.1 hectare, or approximately one-quarter acre). It should be noted that this amount is not equal to total project cost, or length of repayment. See Shibata, "Saitama ken minumadai yōsui ni okeru nōgyō suiri shisutemu" [Agricultural Water-Use System in Minumadai Canal of Saitama Prefecture], chart 8.

[24] *Shichōson* may be translated as "settlement pattern." Three distinctions are possible: *shi*, cities; *chō*, towns; and *son*, villages; the latter might more accurately be labeled "rural townships" since they do not contain a real town of any significance and are composed instead of physical villages and their lands. See Ginsburg, "Economic and Cultural Geography," in *Introduction to Japanese Civilization*: 445-46; and Kornhauser, *Japan*: 32-33.

[25] The numbers following each *shichōson* administrative unit refer to census track number, the basis for place name identification, in maps 5 and 6.

[26] Total hectarage affected by projects for *kukaku seiri*, land consolidation, for each of the five periods is as follows: 5,679 hectares for 1950-54; 9,143 hectares for 1955-59; 6,642 hectares for 1960-64; 9,453 hectares for 1965-69; 6,218 hectares for 1970-81. The thirty-one-year period also includes 1949, a year in which 520 hectares benefited from this type of *tochi kairyō*, land improvement. The fifth period, 1970-81, has a longer time frame than the others because it includes completion of projects begun in 1974.

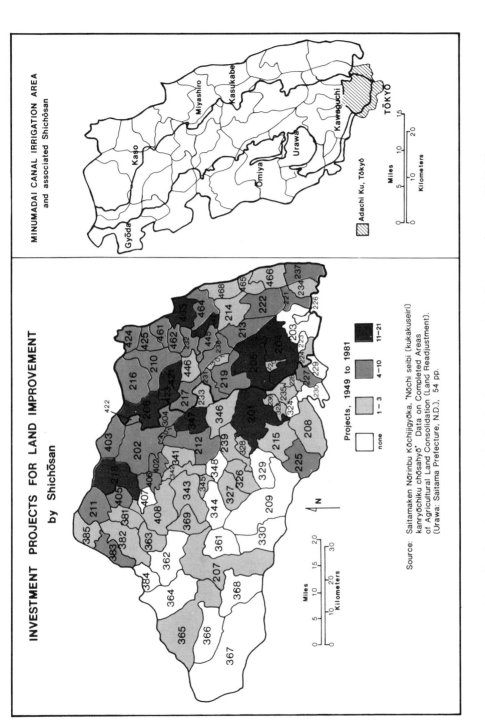

Map 6. *Investment projects for land improvement, Saitama prefecture, 1949-81.*

project location confirms the north/south distinction noted above, and also calls attention to a steadily increasing flow of investment to the north in the post-World War II period; Fukaya-*shi* (#218), located in the north-central part of the prefecture, had a low level of project activity until the middle 1960s, attaining its higher standing primarily owing to LID establishment in the period 1965 through 1969.[27] Temporal analysis also reveals several other noteworthy adjustments between the late 1950s and late 1960s in the characteristics of projects for *kukaku seiri*, land readjustment. They are: growth in average project size, from 93 to 114 hectares; a dramatic increase in the number of projects for farmland replotment at the scale of 30 *āru*, so that by 1969 fully 80.7 percent of all investment was at this scale; and an appreciable change in the amount of farmland reorganized specifically for *hatake nōgyō*, dry-field agriculture, shifting from 27.3 to 43.9 percent.[28]

Increases in the scale of replotment clearly reflect the influence of legislation for promoting mechanization of agricultural production at the field level through *hojō seibi*, farmland consolidation. However, an important qualification should be made regarding the popularity of this post-1964 consolidation standard for land improvement in Saitama. Closer investigation indicates that while over 80.7 percent of land improvement between 1965 and 1969 took place at the scale of 30 *āru*, such investment was promoted by less than one-half of all LIDs, 40.9 percent, during this five-year block of time. In addition, fewer than one-third of these projects for larger-scale agricultural production can be classified technically as *hojō seibi*, which includes underdrainage and other site-level modifications considered fundamental to increasing the efficiency of agricultural production, as distinct from

---

[27] Before 1965, the number of projects in Fukaya-*shi* (#218) for *kukaku seiri*, land readjustment, or *hojō seibi*, farmland consolidation, totaled only three. In the period 1965-69, eight projects were executed. An additional project took place in the period 1970-81.

[28] The land investment and land-use trends described here generally parallel the changing farming conditions in Saitama prefecture between 1950 and 1982, as reflected by census data. In 1955, 63 percent of all farmers in Saitama were *sengyō noka*, full-time farm households; this total had dropped to 20 percent by 1965, 12.2 percent by 1975, and 9.5 percent by 1982. In approximately the same time, 1955-81, the total amount of arable land dropped by 31 percent, from 160,000 hectares to 111,000 hectares; as a percentage of arable land use, wet-paddy declined precipitously from 38 to 20 percent, while vegetable production shot up from 12 to 31 percent, and livestock production from 16 to 29 percent. The degree of agricultural mechanization is equally remarkable; between 1960 and 1974, rice cultivators increased over four-fold, from 2,000 units to 8,500 units, and rice planters and rice harvesters jumped from zero to 17,000 and 21,000 units, respectively, between 1965 and 1974. Sources: Saitama Ken, *Saitama no tochi kairyō* [Land Improvement in Saitama], 1977: 19-41; Saitama Ken, *Saitama ken no tochi kairyō (jigyō gaiyō)* [Land Improvement in Saitama Prefecture (Project Summary)], 1981 and 1983: 25-37; and Saitama Ken Nōrinbu, *Saitama no nōrinsuisangyō, 1981 and 1983* [Agriculture, Forestry and Fishery Production in Saitama, 1981 and 1983] (Urawa: Saitama Ken, 1981 and 1983): 1-30; 47-73. Cf. chapter 2, especially charts 1 and 2.

kukaku seiri, which does not necessarily include establishment of an under-drainage network. Average project size for larger-scale land replotment was nearly double the prefecture average for all *kukaku seiri* projects, at 224.5 hectares. A final observation is that of the thirty-four larger-scale projects initiated during this time frame only two were located in the southern half of the prefecture. The exceptions, Urawa-*shi* (#204)/ Ōmiya-*shi* (#205) and Ina-*machi* (#301), totaled only 92 hectares, a mere 1.2 percent of all such land improvement.[29]

These observations about replotment may be summarized either from the perspective of the entire thirty-one years under study, or from that of the decade and a half after promulgation of legislation for *hojō seibi,* farmland consolidation. In terms of the period from 1949 to 1981, approximately one out of every three hectares, 37.6 percent, was replotted at the 30 *āru* scale, a figure that can be contrasted to the total number of LIDs engaged in such activity, less than one in five, 18.6 percent. Slightly over one-quarter of these projects, 28 percent, were for *hojō seibi,* covering 63.6 percent of the hectares in the prefecture benefiting from such land improvement activity. Isolation of the period from 1965 to 1981 changes these statistics some-what.[30] In this time, approximately four out of every five hectares, 80.5 percent, were replotted at a scale of 30 *āru,* and two out of every five LIDs, 40.1 percent, promoted such land improvement. During the post-1965 period slightly over one-third of all projects, 34.4 percent, were for *hojō seibi,* covering 71.3 percent of farmland benefiting from such investment. Further analysis of these statistics, in terms of project distribution during the years 1965 to 1981, indicates that only six projects, 9.8 percent, covering 423 hectares, or 3.3 percent of 30 *āru* farmland replotment, were located in the southern half of Saitama prefecture;[31] in contrast, the twenty-one *hojō seibi* projects initiated at this time were located exclusively in the northern half of Saitama prefecture.

---

[29] It should be underscored that there was an overall decline in the number of projects for *kukaku seiri,* land readjustment, to the south, but an increase to the north and northwest, from 1965 through 1974.

[30] Given the fact that legislation for *hojō seibi jigyō,* farmland consolidation projects, was enacted in 1964, the shift of time frame gives a more accurate picture of such activity in Saitama prefecture.

[31] Mr. Yamamoto Shigeo, (then) assistant section chief, Kōchi Keikakuka, Nōrinbu, Saitama prefecture, pointed out to the author in an interview in 1983 that his office had worked quite hard to convince farmers in Ōmiya-*shi* (#205) to replot their land at the scale of 30 *āru* (.3 hectare), but had had extremely limited success. Data analysis from 1965 to 1981 confirms this observation; fewer than 50 hectares, representing one project, were reorganized at this larger scale in Ōmiya-*shi.*

The implications of this review of the characteristics of projects for *kukaku seiri*, land readjustment, are severalfold. LIDs promoting this particular type of infrastructure investment in Saitama prefecture have varied over time and space, and have also experienced changes in function during the thirty-one-year period from 1949 to 1981. Two factors seem to have influenced adjustments in project location, size, scale, and objectives. One factor, as already noted, was promulgation of the *Nōgyō Kihon Hō*, Agricultural Basic Law of 1961, which established the framework for promoting projects for *hojō seibi*, farmland consolidation. The objectives of such policy include modification of those site-level conditions that interfere with crop production, through upgrading of facilities for water control, distribution, and drainage, as well as replotment of irregularly shaped fields, in order to encourage the mechanization and diversification of Japanese agriculture. A second factor influencing *kukaku seiri* activity has been the degree of urbanization in the southern portions of the prefecture. As Saitama experienced regional specialization of cash crop production, in large part to meet the needs of the burgeoning Tokyo market, land improvement projects for *hatake nōgyō*, dry-field agriculture, have shown a marked increase. In short, owing to changes of policy, and to the social and economic forces related to urbanization, Saitama displays a pattern of *kukaku seiri* investment with centers of LID activity both in the northern and southern portions of the prefecture. These dual centers of investment display radically different characteristics: to the north, larger-scale projects are dominant, in both total area and replotment size; to the south, projects are considerably smaller in scale. Both centers of production display increasing amounts of *hatake nōgyō* land improvement.

The magnitude of *hojō seibi*, farmland consolidation, deserves careful explanation in the context of these general observations. Between 1949 and 1981 approximately one out of four hectares were so developed; the total shifts to more than one out of every two hectares for the period 1965 to 1981. Despite this doubling in the hectarage affected, the Saitama prefecture *Nōrinbu*, Agricultural Department, reported that as of 1980, *hojō seibi* improvements had been completed on only 28 percent of all arable land being promoted for agricultural use. This statistic leads to a significant conclusion regarding Saitama prefecture, that it is relatively advanced in *kukaku seiri*, but backward in *hojō seibi*.[32]

---

[32] Saitama Ken Nōrinbu, *Saitama no nōrinsuisangyō* [Agriculture, Forestry and Fishery Production in Saitama]: 28. There is a remarkable similarity between the percentage of arable land benefiting from farmland consolidation projects, *hojō seibi jigyō*, at the national level, 33 percent, and in Saitama, 28 percent. The reasons for this in the Saitama case appear to be two-fold: (1) significant amounts of investment in the agricultural infrastructure took place during the Tokugawa and Meiji periods; and (2) the heterogenous nature of farmland ownership split among vassals of the Tokugawa shogunate, the shogunate itself, and territory owned by religious temples and shrines. Scattered holdings in particular do not bode

Pattern of Irrigation Development in Saitama:
The Case of the Minumadai Irrigation Canal

This survey of infrastructure investment in Saitama prefecture has so far concentrated on land improvement projects for *kukaku seiri*, land readjustment. Attention will now shift to discussion of the irrigation network; the specific object of analysis in this case will be the Minuma LID,[33] the organization with responsibility for *iji kanri*, irrigation and drainage canal maintenance, on the main stem of the Minumadai irrigation canal. The areal characteristics of the canal, including its north/south orientation and its location relative to the Tokyo metropolitan area, are displayed on maps 3 through 9.

The Minuma LID is one of more than 100 irrigation organizations with maintenance responsibilities established throughout Saitama prefecture in the late 1940s and early 1950s. This period of time represents the first of two stages in the evolution of post-World War II land improvement projects. The second stage, which extends to the present, has been shaped by legislative decisions as well as rapidly changing social and economic conditions, leading to increasing demands for rationalization of water use in agricultural areas. The specific pieces of legislation that have had the most profound influence on the operation of *iji kanri* LIDs in this second stage are the *Mizu Shigen Kaihatsu Sokushin Hō*, Water Resources Development Promotion Law of 1961, and the *Kasen Hō*, River Law of 1964. Their effect, in combination with widespread urbanization pressures, will be discussed below with reference to efforts to promote projects for *nōgyō yōsui gōrika*, agricultural water-use rationalization, in the Minumadai irrigation network.

---

well for the consensus needed for *hojō seibi* projects. See Shibata, "Saitama ken minumadai yōsui ni okeru nōgyō suiri shisutemu" [Agricultural Water-Use System in Minumadai Canal of Saitama Prefecture], maps 1-4.

[33] The name of the Minuma LID went through a number of changes after establishment on August 2, 1952. Since 1967 it has been designated legally as the Minuma LID; its primary function is to assume responsibility for *iji kanri*, irrigation and drainage canal maintenance, on the main stem of the Minumadai canal. See Minuma Tochi Kairyō Ku, *Minuma tochi kairyō ku teikan* [Minuma LID Articles of Incorporation] (Urawa: Minuma Tochi Kairyō Ku, n.d.): 1, for a summary of the purpose and management responsibilities of the Minuma LID. It should be underscored that the definition of *iji kanri* responsibilities for the Minuma LID pertain only to the main canal. It should also be noted that the terms "Minuma LID" and "Minumadai canal irrigation area" are to be distinguished from each other; the former refers to an institution, a LID, based on the obligations and benefits accruing to those who are paying members of this administrative organization.

The Minumadai Canal

The Minumadai irrigation canal stretches in a north-south direction for some sixty kilometers across the central portion of the Kantō plain. To the north, the canal taps the Tone River as its primary irrigation source, at the *Tone ōzeki*, a large-scale headworks facility located in Gyōda-*shi*, Saitama prefecture.[34] To the south, the canal extends into Adachi-*ku*,[35] Tokyo prefecture, a densely settled, heavily urbanized area abutting the Ara River.[36] The canal's relative location is presented in map 7. Canal history can be traced to 1728, making it one of the oldest large-scale irrigation networks in the Kantō.[37] The administrative organization with responsibility for water distribution in the Minumadai canal irrigation area, the Minuma LID, can be ranked as one of the single largest irrigation organizations in Japan. As of 1979 it had a beneficiary area of 13,102.7 hectares, with membership totaling 26,533 people.[38]

---

[34] A sketch of the *Tone ōzeki*, the modern intake point of the Minumadai irrigation canal, can be found in Latz, *Nihon ni okeru kangai* [Irrigation in Japan]: 70.

[35] Adachi-*ku* is one of the twenty-three political-administrative subdivisions (wards) of the City of Tokyo.

[36] The relative location of the Tokyo metropolitan area to the southern portion of the Minumadai canal is summarized in maps 3, 4, 7, and 8.

[37] The Minumadai irrigation canal has been the subject of a large number of historical studies, in large part owing to its size; age; utilization of sophisticated agricultural civil engineering techniques; traditional dual function as an irrigation and rice transportation network, *tsūsen bori*; and the importance of the area to the *bakufu*, Japanese feudal government, during the Tokugawa period, 1603 to 1867. A cross-section of references follows: Minumadai Yōsui Tochi Kairyō Ku, ed., *Minumadai yōsui enkakushi* [The Historical Development of Minumadai Irrigation Canal] (Urawa: Minumadai Yōsui Tochi Kairyō Ku, 1957); Saitama Ken, *Saitama no tochi kairyō*, 1977: 75-114; Minuma Tochi Kairyō Ku, *Minumadai yōsui kaihatsu 250 nen kinen--shiori* [The 250th Anniversary of the Development of the Minumadai Irrigation Canal--Handbook] (Urawa: Minuma Tochi Kairyō Ku, 1977); Shinzawa Kagato, *Nōgyō suiri ron* [A Study of Irrigation] (Tokyo: Tokyo Daigaku Shuppan Kai, 1955, reissued 1980): 241-356; Shinzawa Kagato, *Tochi kairyō ron* [A Study of Land Improvement] (Tokyo: Tokyo Daigaku Shuppan Kai, 1955); Shimura Hiroyasu, "Minumadai yōsui" [Minumadai Irrigation Canal], *Nihon no Kagaku to Gijutsu '79/Maikurokonputa*: 90-96; Ina Yoshihiko, "Minumadai yōsui no oitachi" [Historical Background of the Minumadai Irrigation Canal]; and Shibata, "Saitama ken minumadai yōsui ni okeru nōgyō suiri shisutemu" [Agricultural Water-Use System in Minumadai Canal of Saitama Prefecture]: 3-4. There is a good English-language summary of Shinzawa, *Nōgyō suiri ron*, in Kelly, *Irrigation Management in Japan*: 20-23.

[38] These figures are based on the following sources: Minumadai Tochi Kairyō Ku, *Minumadai yōsuiro tochi kairyō ku iji kanri keikakusho* [Planning Documents for Irrigation and Drainage Maintenance of the Minumadai Irrigation Canal] (Urawa: Minumadai Tochi Kairyō Ku, 1952); and Minuma Tochi Kairyo Ku, *Tsūjō sōdaikai gian* [Regular Representative Sessions] (Urawa: Minuma Tochi Kairyo Ku, annual, 1953 through 1980). The summary

The location of the Minumadai canal, within the Kantō plain, between two major rivers, and adjacent to and overlapping with Japan's single largest metropolitan area, suggests the complex environmental[39] and socioeconomic forces shaping operation of this irrigation network. One example of this point is that urban and agricultural land-use patterns differ dramatically from south to north in the Minumadai canal irrigation area, as indicated by a comparison of population density in Gyōda-*shi* and Kawaguchi-*shi*.[40] These two areas of Saitama prefecture are approximately equal in total size but radically different in terms of total population, with the latter some six times larger as of 1980, classifying it as a densely inhabited district (DID) of 4,000 people or more per square kilometer. Such high population densities have a direct effect on the amount of land converted

---

comment in the text is adapted from Shibata, "Daitoshi kinko ni okeru nōgyō suiri soshiki no henyō" [Evolution and Response of Agricultural Water-Use Organizations to Suburbanization and the Demand for Water Rationalization], table 7, p. 5.

[39] The environmental complexity of the area under study is illustrated by maps 3 and 7. Map 3 calls attention to the alluvial nature of the Kantō region. Map 7 directs the reader's attention to the location of Shibayama and Kawarabuki inverted siphons. Of the many obstacles to smooth transfer of water from river or reservoir to the wet-paddy field, the problem of circumventing a river course is one of the most technically complicated. In the case of the Shibayama inverted siphon, water is conducted under the bed of the Moto Ara River; a sketch of this water conveyance technique can be found in Latz, *Nihon ni okeru kangai* [Irrigation in Japan]: 71. Another alternative is construction of a water bridge, but its susceptibility to flood damage is a severe limitation.

[40] Gyōda-*shi* (census #206) and Kawaguchi-*shi* (census #203) measure, respectively, 60.8 square kilometers and 55.7 square kilometers; a comparison of population reveals that according to the 1980 census, the former had 73,205 people while the latter had 379,360 people. Cartographic representation of the location and population characteristics of these two administrative units can be found in maps 5 and 8.
    DIDs in Saitama prefecture, measured in terms of *shichōson* with 4,000 people or more per square kilometer, include: Kawaguchi-*shi* (#203), Urawa-*shi* (#204), Kasukabe-*shi* (#214), Yono-*shi* (#220), Sōka-*shi* (#221), Warabi-*shi* (#223), Toda-*shi* (#224), Hatogaya-*shi* (#226), Asaka-*shi* (#227), Shiki-*shi* (#228), Wakō-*shi* (#229), Niiza-*shi* (#230), Fujimi-*shi* (#235), Kamifukuoka-*shi* (#236), and Ōi-*machi* (#322). The population for the prefecture increased 12.4 percent between 1975 and 1980, expanding from 4,821,340 to 5,420,480; of this total, more than 50 percent live in areas designated as DIDs, which in turn occupy only 13.5 percent of the prefecture. Of these DIDs, Kasukabe-*shi* (#214) had the highest rate of population growth between 1975 and 1980, increasing by 27.9 percent. Additional *shichoson* that are within 1,000 people of being classified as DIDs, that is, have population densities in excess of 3,000 people per square kilometer, include: Ōmiya-*shi* (#205), Tokorozawa-*shi* (#208), Ageo-*shi* (#219), Koshigaya-*shi* (#222), Yashio-*shi* (#234), and Misato-*shi* (#237). The *shichōson* with the highest total population in Saitama prefecture is Kawaguchi-*shi*, with 379,360 people; this figure may be compared to Adachi-*ku*, Tokyo, the southern terminus of the Minumadai irrigation canal, which is estimated to have a population of 606,104 people. See Nihon, Sorifu Tōkeikyoku, *Showa 55 nen, waga kuni no jinkō shūchū chiku* [Concentrated Population Districts of the Nation, 1980].

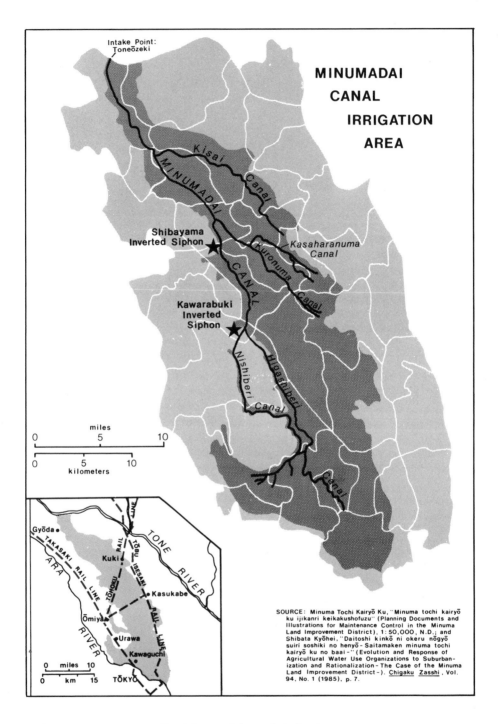

Intake Point:
Toneōzeki

MINUMADAI
CANAL
IRRIGATION
AREA

Kisai Canal

MINUMADAI

Shibayama
Inverted Siphon

Kasaharanuma Canal

Kuronuma Canal

CANAL

Kawarabuki
Inverted
Siphon

Nishiberi Canal

Higashiberi Canal

miles
0   5   10

0   5   10
kilometers

Gyōda

Kuki

TONE RIVER

TAKASAKI RAIL LINE

ARA RIVER

TŌHOKU RAIL LINE

ŌBU ISESAKI

Kasukabe

Ōmiya

Urawa

Kawaguchi

TŌKYŌ

0   miles   10

0   km   15

SOURCE: Minuma Tochi Kairyō Ku, "Minuma tochi kairyō
ku ijikanri keikakushofuzu" (Planning Documents and
Illustrations for Maintenance Control in the Minuma
Land Improvement District), 1:50,000, N.D.; and
Shibata Kyōhei, "Daitoshi kinkō ni okeru nōgyō
suiri soshiki no henyō-Saitamaken minuma tochi
kairyō ku no baai-" (Evolution and Response of
Agricultural Water Use Organizations to Suburbanization and Rationalization-The Case of the Minuma
Land Improvement District-). <u>Chigaku</u> <u>Zasshi</u>, Vol.
94, No. 1 (1985). p. 7.

Map 7: Minumadai canal irrigation area.

from agricultural to urban uses, and between the late 1950s and the late 1970s there was an estimated loss of one-quarter of the total Minuma LID irrigation beneficiary area, and a loss of an estimated 3,500 paying LID members.[41] Despite the intensity of urbanization pressures in the southern portions of the Minuma LID, however, it is remarkable that the total area and number of participating farmers have remained relatively constant in the post-World War II period, as converted farmland to the south has been replaced by amalgamation of formerly distinct irrigation networks to the north.[42] These points are summarized by map 8, which illustrates the state of suburban land-use pressures, in terms of population density in the southern portion of the canal,[43] as well as the location of the most recently amalgamated *iji kanri* LID to the north, Kisai irrigation canal.[44]

The information organized by map 8 offers several insights into the state of agricultural activity in Saitama prefecture. Of particular importance to the present discussion is that there has been a wholesale shift of agricultural activity in the post-World War II period to the north; to the south, in contrast, the agricultural water-use and drainage functions of the canal have virtually ceased as a result of heavy urbanization.[45] This

---

[41] Loss of agricultural land is estimated to have averaged 200 hectares per year, reaching a peak in the late 1960s at 300 hectares per year. A decline in the number of members also reached a peak in the late 1960s. These estimates are based on the sources found in note 38.

[42] Hectarage lost, 1952 through 1979, totaled 4,812.3 hectares, almost exactly equal to amalgamated land, totaling 4,794.5 hectares. Total area and membership during the same time actually increased slightly, moving from a base of 12,738.5 to 13,102.7 hectares, and from 24,251 to 26,533 people. These estimates are based on the sources found in note 38.

[43] Only the amalgamation of Kisai *iji kanri* LID is shown on map 8; omitted are four other areas amalgamated between 1962 and 1979. For complete cartographic and tabular representation of land-use changes, see Shibata, "Daitoshi kinkō ni okeru nōgyō suiri soshiki no henyō" [Evolution and Response of Agricultural Water-Use Organizations to Suburbanization and Demand for Water Rationalization], table 2, p. 5; and map 1, p. 7.

[44] Kisai, the *iji kanri* LID most recently absorbed into the Minumadai beneficiary area, is a prime example of how the loss of agricultural land to the south has been balanced, in gross statistical terms, through amalgamation to the north. The amalgamation of the Kisai *iji kanri* LID took place in 1983 (and thus is not included in the summary statistics found in notes 41 and 42, which cover the period 1952 to 1979). Prefectural information indicates that Kisai had a membership of 3,519 farmers and a total area of 1,762 hectares as of 1982. See Saitama Ken Nōrinbu Kōchikeikakuka, *Showa 57 shigatsu tsuitachi genzai tochi kairyō ku meibo* [April 1, 1982, Register of Land Improvement Districts] (Urawa: Saitama Ken, 1982).

[45] My inspection of the southern portion of the canal in 1982 revealed that it functions primarily for sewage disposal for the surrounding *shichōson*. For more on such (new) water-use charges levied by the Minuma LID on these southern *shichōson*, see Shibata, "Daitoshi kinkō ni okeru nōgyō suiri soshiki no henyō" [Evolution and Response of Agricultural Water-Use Organizations to Suburbanization and the Demand for Water Rationalization]: 10-15.

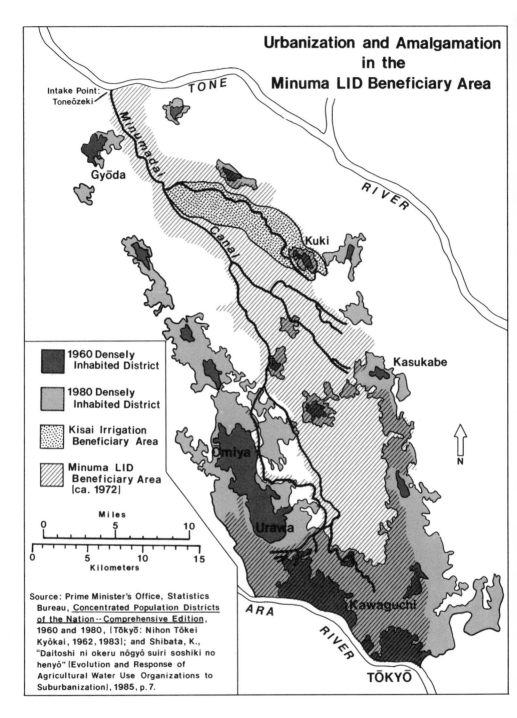

Urbanization and Amalgamation in the Minuma LID Beneficiary Area

Intake Point: Toneōzeki

TONE

Minumadai

Gyōda

Canal

Kuki

RIVER

Kasukabe

1960 Densely Inhabited District

1980 Densely Inhabited District

Kisai Irrigation Beneficiary Area

Minuma LID Beneficiary Area [ca. 1972]

Omiya

Miles
0   5   10

0   5   10   15
Kilometers

Urawa

N

Source: Prime Minister's Office, Statistics Bureau, Concentrated Population Districts of the Nation -- Comprehensive Edition, 1960 and 1980, [Tōkyō: Nihon Tōkei Kyōkai, 1962, 1983]; and Shibata, K., "Daitoshi ni okeru nōgyō suiri soshiki no henyō" [Evolution and Response of Agricultural Water Use Organizations to Suburbanization], 1985, p. 7.

ARA

Kawaguchi

RIVER

TŌKYŌ

Map 8.   Urbanization and amalgamation in the Minuma LID beneficiary area.

observation calls attention to the need to clarify use of the term *jueki chiku*, benefited area, when describing contemporary Japanese irrigation networks experiencing rapid suburbanization. This point will be discussed below with regard to the institutional, areal, and financial meanings of the term.

The Minumadai Canal and the Minuma LID Beneficiary Area

From a legal and institutional point of view, the *jueki chiku*, benefited area, is to be defined in terms of the relationship between those responsible for and those benefiting from water distribution; this relationship is usually maintained through a system of membership dues and obligatory rights to perform maintenance tasks.[46] However, this institutional meaning is often confused with definition of the irrigation network from a technical, engineering viewpoint (i.e., one that places emphasis on the physical extent of the canal structure). The distinction here is between description of the irrigation network in terms of its engineering objective, which is to distribute water, and its institutional objective, which is both to assign responsibility for canal maintenance and to collect monies from the beneficiaries of water distribution. Cartographic presentation of *jueki chiku* can thus take two forms, delimiting either the physical extent of water distribution or the location of paying beneficiaries affiliated with a given LID.[47] These two beneficiary areas are not necessarily the same, and the latter is the more accurate reflection of the current pattern of agricultural land use, and agricultural water demand, in the case of the Minuma LID.[48]

---

[46] This definition is based in part on comments made by David M. Freeman, Colorado State University, in a working session, "Social Considerations in the Planning and Operation of Irrigation Systems," at the Tenth Technical Conference on Irrigation, Drainage, and Flood Control, November 13-16, 1985, in Reno, Nevada. See also D. M. Freeman and Max K. Lowdermilk, "Middle-level Organizational Linkages in Irrigation Projects," in *Putting People First: Sociological Variables in Rural Development*, ed. Michael M. Cernea (New York: Oxford University Press, 1985): 52-90.

[47] One qualification here is that *kengyō nōka*, part-time farm households, may have peculiar water demands, primarily on weekends, that can cause serious problems in the timely provision of water throughout the irrigation network. In short, to be a paying beneficiary may denote the location of water demand, but not necessarily the temporal pattern of water demand.

[48] The physical and social distinctions possible when defining irrigation networks are recognized implicitly in the research of Kelly, *Irrigation Management in Japan*: v-vi, and are discussed explicitly in the research of Shibata, "Daitoshi kinkō ni okeru nōgyō suiri soshiki no henyō" [Evolution and Response of Agricultural Water-Use Organizations to Suburbanization and Demand for Water Rationalization]: 4-9. The *jueki chiku*, benefited area, of the Minuma LID can be identified from an institutional perspective in map 8.

The implications of this distinction between the institutional and engineering meanings of the *jueki chiku* are severalfold. For example, the Kisai irrigation canal discussed previously becomes significant not only as a representative of physical amalgamation, but as an example of overlap between various institutions for irrigation, each with a separate beneficiary area. Further analysis indicates that in this particular case amalgamation has not led to redefinition of the outer limits of the Minuma LID beneficiary area, which have remained relatively constant since 1972.[49] The reason that Kisai has functioned as a distinct organization for water distribution within the Minuma LID beneficiary area is that throughout the entire post-World War II period there has been rigid division of maintenance responsibilities between the main canal and the branch canals of the Minumadai irrigation network, with the former being the exclusive domain of the Minuma LID, and the latter being under the control of twenty-five separate *iji kanri* LIDs, with Kisai representing one of the total number.[50] The complexity of the relationship between the main and the branch canal's LIDs is represented by map 9, which identifies eight overlapping *iji kanri* LIDs within one part of the northern section of the Minuma LID beneficiary area.[51]

---

[49] Cartographic representation of this point can be found in map 8; the northeastern boundary of the Minumadai beneficiary area coincides exactly with that of the Kisai beneficiary area.

[50] The identification and mapping of these twenty-five *iji kanri* LIDs was based on review of unpublished archival materials regarding maintenance plans for LIDs in Saitama prefecture, collected at the Saitamakenchō, Urawa, between 1981 and 1983. Their continuing existence is due primarily to the granting of legal status to traditional *kankō suiri ken*, customary water rights, in 1964. A comprehensive reproduction of all twenty-five *iji kanri* LIDs can be found in Shibata, "Saitama ken minumadai yōsui ni okeru nōgyō suiri shisutemu" [Agricultural Water-Use System of Minumadai Canal of Saitama Prefecture], map 8. Map 9 of this paper is an adaptation of this map.

[51] The degree of irrigation boundary overlap explains the reason Saitama has the greatest degree of accumulated hectarage in the Kantō plain, 22 percent more than the total amount of arable land in the prefecture. In effect, each of the eight areas depicted is counted at least twice in the calculation of total hectarage of *jueki chiku*, benefited areas. The amount of overlap, and number of LIDs in Saitama, is especially significant when considered in light of the level of prefectural investment in *nōgyō kiban seibi*, agricultural infrastructure consolidation, which is considerably below the national average. If projects for *kukaku seiri*, land consolidation, are also considered, a total of seventy-four independent LIDs were operating in or overlapped with the Minuma LID as of 1982; twenty-five of this total were LIDs for *iji kanri*, irrigation and drainage canal maintenance. See Shibata, "Saitama ken minumadai yōsui ni okeru nōgyō suiri shisutemu" [Agricultural Water-Use System in Minumadai Canal of Saitama Prefecture], table 14. A retrospective view indicates that a total of 109 LIDs for *kukaku seiri*, land readjustment, were executed within the Minumadai beneficiary area, 1949 through 1981. See Gil Latz, "*Kukaku seiri*-type Land Improvement Trends in the Minuma LID," unpublished lecture, Graduate Student Seminar, Institute of Human Geography, University of Tokyo, November, 1983.

The picture of amalgamation and overlap thus presented is of a water distribution network within the Minuma LID beneficiary area that is balanced delicately among more than two dozen water-use organizations. The areal integrity of the irrigation canal, then, is severely compromised not only by changes in land use to the south, resulting in diminished canal function, but in terms of the capacity of farmers to participate in projects for land and water-use rationalization, as well as to pay annual assessments for *iji kanri*.[52] To the south this has clearly reached a crisis stage, and the prefecture has taken on more and more responsibility for facility investment and maintenance.[53] To the north, however, a somewhat different financial

---

[52] The annual levy for *iji kanri*, irrigation and drainage maintenance, assessed to members of the Minuma LID had a range of 2,510 yen to 2,660 yen, per hectare, in 1980. Assessments varied from north to south by 150 yen, with costs slightly higher to the south. Three post-World War II trends in levy collection of note are: (1) the levy more than doubled between 1975 and 1980 for all beneficiaries; (2) a high degree of uniformity had been achieved in levy rates, regardless of location in the beneficiary network, by 1980; and (3) there was a remarkable shift in the rate of collection, which stood at 72 percent in 1955 and 96.8 percent in 1980. See Minuma Tochi Kairyō Ku, *Minuma tochi kairyō ku kakunen no sōdaikai gian* [Annual Representative Sessions of the Minuma LID] (Urawa: Minuma Tochi Kairyō Ku, annual since 1953); and Shibata, "Daitoshi kinkō ni okeru nōgyō suiri soshiki no henyō" [Evolution and Response of Agricultural Water-Use Organizations to Suburbanization and Demand for Water Rationalization]: 14.

[53] Prefectural policy, particularly since 1974, has included promotion of *kentandoku jigyō*, independent prefecture-operated projects. These land improvement projects became active in the 1970s owing to the refusal of the *Nōrinsuishanshō*, Ministry of Agriculture, Forestry and Fisheries, to approve project subsidy for smaller-scale LIDs in urbanizing areas; given these circumstances, farmers wishing to promote infrastructure development turned to the prefecture for financial assistance. In the case of the Minumadai beneficiary area, one area in which *kentandoku jigyō*, independent prefecture-operated projects, have been active is south of the Kawarabuki siphon, the location of which is identified in map 7. Ironically, in the midst of this financial crisis leading to greater involvement by the prefecture in infrastructure investment, the Minuma LID began to experience an unprecedented surplus in its budget, due in large part to collection of a *kessai kin*, liquidation levy, assessed against those farmers selling their lands for nonagricultural purposes. The levy is predicated on the projected cost per unit of benefited land for maintenance of the Minumadai irrigation canal for twenty years into the future. Use of these monies is restricted to facilities for protecting against natural hazards, special projects, and servicing of debt repayment to the *Nōrin Gyogyō Kinyū Kōko*, Ministry of Agriculture, Forestry and Fisheries Finance Corporation. As of 1980, the *kessai kin*, liquidation levy, equaled 560,000 yen, or $2,435 per hectare (in 1980 $1 equaled 230 yen), a cost that is usually added on to the land sale price; these levies represented about $2.2 million, one-half of the total Minuma LID budget as of 1980; it should be emphasized that this is a cumulative total and that the amount of *kessai kin* collected in 1980 equaled 4.1 percent of the budget. Even more remarkable is that the levy for *iji kanri*, irrigation and drainage maintenance, represented only 15 percent of the total Minuma LID budget in 1980. See Minuma Tochi Kairyō Ku, *Minuma tochi kairyō ku kakunen sōdaikai gian* [Annual Representative Sessions of the Minuma LID], annual since 1953. Budgetary information is analyzed in considerable detail by Shibata, "Daitoshi kinkō ni okeru nōgyō suiri soshiki no henyō" [Evolution and Response of Agricultural Water-Use Organizations to Suburbanization and Demand for Water Rationalization]: 10-15; note especially p. 11.

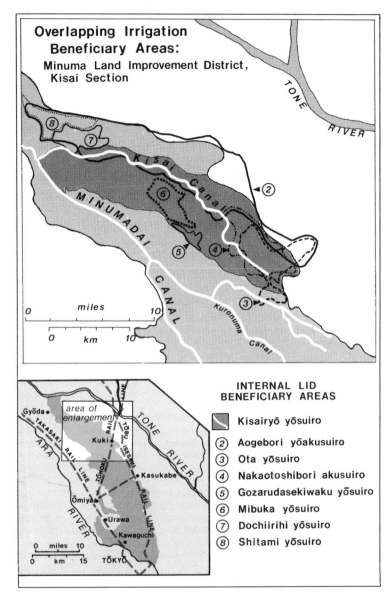

Map 9. *Overlapping irrigation beneficiary areas, Minuma LID, Kisai section.*
Sources: unpublished archival materials regarding maintenance plans for LIDs in Saitama prefecture, Saitamakenchō, Urawa, collected 1981-83; Saitama Ken, Ōmiya Tochi Kairyō Jimusho, "Saitama goguchi nikki jigyō keikaku gaiyō" [Summary Plan for Unification Projects in Saitama], and "Saitama goguchi nikki jigyō keikaku ippan zu" [General Plan for Stage Two Unification Projects]; Saitama Ken, "Ōmiya tochi kairyō jimusho kannai tochi kairyō ku kuiki zu" [Regional Map of LIDs under the Jurisdiction of the Ōmiya Land Improvement Office]; and Shibata, "Saitama ken minumadai yōsui ni okeru nōgyō suiri shisutemu" [Agricultural Water Use System in Minumadai Canal of Saitama Prefecture], map 8.

problem appears. Farmers in the Kisai irrigation area, for example, have paid levy assessments to both the Minuma LID and the Kisai LID for the entire post-World War II period. With amalgamation the costs of irrigation and maintenance fall on fewer and fewer shoulders, while the area to be managed steadily increases, resulting in higher long-range levy assessments.[54] Thus, from an institutional point of view, the costs of amalgamation often exceed the administrative benefits that result from a decline in the amount of overlap within the Minumadai beneficiary area.[55]

The degree of overlap in the Minuma LID beneficiary area becomes an especially serious problem when attempts are made to rationalize agricultural water use in response to changing land-use patterns accompanying suburban activity to the south. Pressure to divert water used historically for agricultural purposes, in direct proportion to the amount of land lost to suburban activity, began in the early 1960s when the *Mizu Shigen Kaihatsu Kōdan*, Water Resource Development Public Corporation, and other administrative organizations first challenged the Minuma LID to curtail its volume of water intake from the Tone River.[56] This attempt at negotiation

---

[54] The proposition that farmers will find it increasingly difficult to pay annual assessments is illustrated by map 9. Let us assume that at present there are 1,000 farmers paying for water-use privileges in this section of the Minuma LID beneficiary area. Each member, regardless of the location of land owned, pays two levies for *iji kanri*, irrigation and drainage canal maintenance, one to the Kisai LID and one to the Minuma LID. The advantage of amalgamation, of course, is that it eliminates one levy. The disadvantage is that maintenance costs will go up for the Minuma LID as the beneficiary area increases; i.e., the main canal maintenance function of Minuma LID will extend to a branch canal maintenance function formerly assumed by the Kisai LID. As this happens, the costs of this increased maintenance will fall on a smaller number of shoulders, since amalgamation has not produced any new, additional membership for the Minuma LID. (It is probable that the amalgamation of the Kisai LID was in anticipation of the long-range inability to collect two levies for *iji kanri*, irrigation and drainage canal maintenance, from Kisai area farmers.)

[55] Perhaps the best example of increased institutional costs due to amalgamation would be the case where a larger or financially healthier LID assumes the repayment debts of a smaller, less financially endowed LID.

[56] The demand that the Minuma LID curtail water intake took place in the context of preparations for the 1964 Olympic Games in Tokyo. By the early 1960s a plan had been formulated to divert 20 cubic meters of water per second from the Tone to the Ara River to meet anticipated increases in water demand associated with development accompanying the Olympic Games. The proposal for achieving this goal was to construct one large water intake facility for six canals then tapping the Tone River. The new facility is now called the *Tone ōzeki*, Tone Headworks, a sketch of which can be found in Latz, *Nihon ni okeru kangai* [Irrigation in Japan]: 70. In addition, a new canal, the Musashi canal, was to be built for diverting this water directly from the Minumadai irrigation canal directly into the Ara River. The project went forward as planned, with the government bearing the high costs associated with headworks construction, estimated to have totaled nearly $35 million. However, the anticipated reduction in agricultural water intake did not occur; the Minuma LID maintained its long-standing *kankō suiri ken*, customary water right, of approximately

was based on the fact that decisions about the alteration of *kankō suiri ken,* customary water rights, had to be deliberated by the elected representatives of the Minuma LID.[57] These negotiations were unsuccessful, however, because the Minuma LID had no authority to reduce intake volume if such action interfered with the volume of water customarily granted to each internal *iji kanri* LID. As a result, and despite widespread recognition that the supply of water exceeded agricultural demands, the legal status of *kankō suiri ken* had the effect of stifling redefinition of the traditional amount of water distributed in the beneficiary area(s).

Since the early 1960s there has been extensive investment in the canal's physical structure, from the headworks to the south, including canal relining and construction of more efficient facilities for water transfer, leading to a projected recapture of 20 cubic meters of water per second previously lost to leakage.[58] The application of technology for *nōgyō yōsui gōrika,* agricultural water-use rationalization,[59] as distinct from actual curtailment of the right to use water, has taken place in two stages. The first stage, beginning in 1962, concentrated on the northern portion of the Minumadai canal, including unification of the headworks and the construction of a new canal for drinking water. The second stage, begun in 1977, is an ongoing project which attempts to control canal water leakage, especially

---

83 cubic meters per second. In effect, the needed water was not to be diverted but recaptured through utilization of more efficient technology to prevent water leakage. See: Mizushigen Kaihatsu Kōdan, "Tone dōsui jigyō gaiyō" [Summary Description of the Tone River Water Conveyance Project] (Tokyo: Mizushigen Kaihatsu Kōdan, 1979), pamphlet; and Hanayama Yuzuru, *Toshi to mizushigen--mizu no seiji keizai gaku* [Cities and Water Resources--The Political Economy of Water] (Tokyo: Kashima Publishing Co., 1977): 93-101.

[57] The legal status of *kankō suiri ken,* customary water rights, was established according to the *Kasen Hō,* River Law of 1964.

[58] A sketch of this leakage-preventing technology can be found in Latz, *Nihon ni okeru kangai* [Irrigation in Japan]: 66. In this case water leakage is controlled by relining the canal with concrete and redesigning those diversion gates that transfer water from the main to the branch canal. The effect of such agricultural infrastructure investment is that it promotes more efficient water transfer at high volume, as well as easier canal maintenance.

[59] The history of post-World War II agricultural water-use rationalization began in Saitama prefecture in 1963, some eight years prior to establishment of national guidelines by the *Nōrinsuisanshō,* Ministry of Agriculture, Forestry and Fisheries, leading to establishment in 1974 of *nōgyō yōsui gōrika jigyō,* agricultural water-use rationalization projects. The absence of an institutional structure for dealing with competing demands for water is probably one of the reasons Minuma LID did not negotiate its *kankō suiri ken,* customary water rights, in the early 1960s. See Saitama Ken, *Saitama no tochi kairyō* [Land Improvement in Saitama], 1977: 145-64.

south of Kawarabuki siphon, as well as to construct a new canal for surplus water, stretching from Ōmiya-*shi* to the Ara River.[60]

The apparently heavy reliance on technology to satisfy nonagricultural water demands, rather than the alternative of reallocating water-use rights, will be discussed further in chapter 5. It is ironic that some 72 percent of Saitama's arable land has yet to receive adequate amounts of investment for *hojō seibi*, farmland consolidation.[61] Water use will probably increase, therefore, as such investment is made, further complicating efforts to promote projects for *nōgyō yōsui gōrika*, agricultural water-use rationalization. Projections can now be made, utilizing complex mathematical equations, about either decreases in agricultural water demand due to urbanization, or corresponding increases in water demand as the degree of water control at the field level is elevated by means of *hojō seibi*.[62] However, an institutional structure for transferring water that is acceptable to urban and agricultural interests has yet to be agreed upon.

This chapter began with the stated purpose of clarifying the operation of the LID in a particular agricultural setting, that of Saitama prefecture. The methodology adopted in this analysis was to consider four types of LIDs, two concerned primarily with the land infrastructure, namely, *kukaku seiri*, land readjustment, and *hojō seibi*, farmland consolidation, and two concerned primarily with the water control network, namely, *iji kanri*, irrigation and drainage canal maintenance, and *nōgyō yōsui gōrika*, agricultural water-use rationalization. The time frame for the discussion cov-

---

[60] The second stage concentrates primarily on the southern portion of the Minumadai irrigation canal, from the Kawarabuki siphon to Ōmiya-*shi*, and from Ōmiya-*shi* to the Ara River. See map 7. Referred to as the *Saitama Goguchi Nikki Jigyō*, the Second Stage of Unification in Saitama, the project aims to transfer 3.1 cubic meters of water per second to the Ara River. Like the *Tone ōzeki* project discussed in note 56, however, this diversion of water from agricultural use will actually be accomplished by increasing the efficiency of the water conveyance network, a literal recapturing of lost water. The project was scheduled for completion in 1985; between 1977 and 1983, project costs totaled $13.5 million. See Saitama Ken, "Saitama goguchi nikki jigyō" [Stage Two Unification Projects]; and Saitama Ken, "Saitama goguchi nikki jigyō zentai keikaku (gaiyō)" [Complete Plans for Stage Two Unification Projects in Saitama (Summary)] (Urawa: Saitama Ken, n.d.).

[61] The percentage of arable land affected by projects for farmland consolidation at the national level, 33 percent, is remarkably similar to the Saitama case, 28 percent. The latter is discussed in Saitama Ken Nōrinbu, *Saitama no nōrinsuisangyō* [Agriculture, Forestry and Fishery Production in Saitama]: 28.

[62] Personal conversations, Mizutani Masakazu, Faculty of Agriculture, Mie University. See also Mizutani Masakazu, "Toshika to nōgyō yōsui" [Urbanization and Agricultural Water-Use], in *Mizu to nihon nōgyō* [Water and Japanese Agriculture], ed. Ogata Hiroyuki (Tokyo: Tokyo Daigaku Shuppan Kai, 1979): 285-305.

ered the period from the late 1940s to the early 1980s, some three decades in which national-level changes in legislation, and local-level changes in the nonagricultural population, combined to redefine the objectives of land improvement policies in Saitama, particularly in the southern portions of the prefecture.

Two stages of policy adjustments, emphasizing rationalization of land and water use at the site level, together with urbanization pressures, had the effect of creating two zones of high LID activity, one to the north and one to the south, in the case of *kukaku seiri* LIDs, and a shift in the center of agricultural water-use investment to the northern portion of the Minumadai canal, in the case of the Minuma *iji kanri* LID. Of particular interest was the attempt during the post-World War II period to reallocate *kankō suiri ken*, customary water rights, as land conversion occurred to the south; this did not materialize, owing to the complex relationship between the Minuma LID and twenty-five separate and often overlapping *iji kanri* LIDs within its beneficiary area. The reason for such resistance to agricultural water-use rationalization, *nōgyō yōsui gōrika*, is that each internal LID acts as an independent representative for legally established *kankō suiri ken*, customary water rights, in a given irrigation network, and the appropriate institutional structure for negotiations regarding the reallocation of these rights has yet to be developed.

Physical, social, and economic conditions have each had an effect on the distribution of LIDs in Saitama over the course of the post-World War II period. The degree to which site conditions have influenced the pattern of investment is especially striking when viewed in terms of the concepts on which land improvement policy is based. The Saitama case, as reviewed here, is clearly at odds with the stated goal of this investment program, to promote coordinated development of the agricultural infrastructure. Saitama does not display a "coordinated" pattern of development when viewed either from the perspective of the prefecture-wide distribution of LIDs for *kukaku seiri*, land readjustment, or from that of the specific operations of Minuma LID for *iji kanri*, irrigation and drainage canal maintenance. This is well illustrated by the surprisingly small number of LIDs for either *hojō seibi*, farmland consolidation, or *nōgyō yōsui gōrika*, agricultural water-use rationalization; in both respects Saitama may be said to lack clear vision about the future role of agriculture in the prefecture. The absence of coordinated development is also illustrated from a linguistic point of view, since the administrative terminology for infrastructure investment--i.e., *hojō seibi*, farmland consolidation; *kukaku seiri*, land readjustment; *nōgyō yōsui gōrika*, agricultural water-use rationalization-- does not reflect clearly the improvement activities with which they are engaged. The same point can be made if one considers the preceding discussion of LIDs for *iji kanri* and *kukaku seiri* found within the Minumadai canal irrigation area. There is no institutional structure that grants the Minuma LID the authority to promote rationalization of land and water use based on a clearly established definition of the beneficiary area for the Minumadai irrigation network.

In short, the articulation of a policy goal aiming at comprehensive development of the agricultural infrastructure has not necessarily had the effect of creating coordinated development and rationalization of land and water use in the primary sector of Saitama prefecture. The main reason for this failure of policy in practice appears to be that land improvement programs do not actively challenge prevailing attitudes about traditional customary water rights, *kankō suiri ken*, despite dynamic changes in non-agricultural land utilization within or adjacent to the areal unit covered by a given irrigation network. In fact, the opposite seems to have occurred in the case of the *iji kanri*, irrigation and drainage canal maintenance, LIDs; increasingly these organizations have assumed the role of representing and protecting agricultural water-use rights in response to reallocation pressures from other sectors of the regional economy in the Kantō plain. The implications of these observations will be discussed further in chapter 5.

Chapter 5

FINDINGS AND OBSERVATIONS

The objective of this research has been to assess the role of Japanese government policies for investment in the agricultural infrastructure in the post-World War II period. Scrutiny of these policies began with review of the terminology peculiar to government and government-related literature which describes and analyzes such investment programs, focusing on the concept of *tochi kairyō*, land improvement (introduction and chapter 1). Investigation then proceeded to a summary description of the environmental and socioeconomic features of Japan's primary sector (chapter 2), followed by identification of the characteristics of land improvement policy and its evolution over the course of the twentieth century (chapter 3). The pattern of infrastructure investment resulting from land improvement projects was evaluated further in terms of a particular case study, that of Saitama prefecture, where the distribution and functions of *Tochi Kairyō Ku*, Land Improvement Districts, were considered both on a prefecture-wide basis and in terms of a specific irrigation network, the Minumadai irrigation canal (chapter 4). In this final chapter the perspective will change to one of summary and overview regarding the postwar Japanese policy for land improvement.

I have argued that language--its usage, conceptual meaning, and the visual image that it conveys--is of fundamental importance to the study of land improvement policy in post-World War II Japan. Translation problems confronting the foreign student of Japanese agricultural development policy illustrate this point, setting the stage for final commentary on the LID in concept and practice.

A complex level of confusion in the Japanese literature, and one that has direct bearing on the findings of the research project, is a disconcerting amount of ambiguity in the definitions of terms specific to policy programs for the modernization of the contemporary agricultural production system. In the course of literature review, one confronts an amorphous administrative jargon, particularly with reference to such policy-related designations as: *hojō seibi*, farmland consolidation; *kōchi seiri*, arable land reorganization; *kukaku seiri*, land readjustment; *tochi kairyō*, land improvement; *nōgyō kōzō kaizen*, agricultural structure improvement; *nōgyō kiban seibi*, agricultural infrastructure consolidation; and *nōgyō yōsui gōrika*, agricultural water-use rationalization. The first four of these terms are often used interchangeably to describe the reorganization of agricultural areas through construction of irrigation and drainage facilities, or reshaping of field parcels (with or without underdrainage), in order to realize various goals linked to attempts to increase the efficiency of agricultural production in Japan. A case in point is the Japanese *Kōchi Seiri Hō*, Arable Land Reorganization Law of 1899, which, in the author's opinion, is translated incorrectly as the Arable Land Replotment Law, the Arable Land Consolidation Law, or the Cultivated Land Readjustment Law. An attempt has been made in the preceding discussion to clarify important differences between such terms with reference to the objectives of a variety of legislative programs.[1]

The problem of translation and meaning is mirrored by the fact that most texts on Japanese agriculture fail to include well-designed illustrations of domestic irrigation or land improvement projects. Even in those cases where illustrations can be found, they are often constructed sloppily, usually without reference to scale, and are frequently devoid of a legend that clearly indicates what is being depicted. This is a vexing problem, especially for the foreign researcher, since the dearth of illustrations makes visual clarification of the objectives of land improvement policy extremely difficult. This point seems to be of such basic importance that it will be used as an organ-

---

[1] See also Latz, *Nihon ni okeru kangai* [Irrigation in Japan]. Note the separate definitions for: Arable Land Reorganization Law, *Kōchi Seiri Hō*; land improvement, *tochi kairyō*; land readjustment, *kukaku seiri*; land improvement project, *tochi kairyō jigyō*; farmland consolidation, *hojō seibi*; farmland consolidation project, *hojō seibi jigyō*; agricultural structure improvement project, *nōgyō kōzō kaizen jigyō*; and agricultural water-use rationalization project, *nōgyō yōsui gōrika jigyō*. The general messiness of the administrative terminology, as one Japanese scholar has put it, can be deciphered through reference to the following sources: Shirai, *Nihon no kōchi seibi* [Land Improvement in Japan]: 2, particularly the definition of "land improvement" (and the distinction made there between academic and bureaucratic usage of this term); Shibata, "Nōgyō suiri no shisutemu" [Agricultural Water-Use System]: 65-68, particularly the definition of "land improvement project"; Shibata, "Saitama ken minumadai yōsui ni okeru nōgyō suiri shisutemu" [Agricultural Water-Use System of Minumadai Canal of Saitama Prefecture]: 1, 2, 4, particularly the definitions of "land improvement" and "agricultural infrastructure consolidation project"; Ogura, ed., *Agricultural Development*: 238-46; Kiuchi Shinzo, ed., *Geography in Japan* (Tokyo: Tokyo University Press, Special Publication no. 3, Association of Japanese Geographers, 1976): 120-23; and Ogura, *Can Japanese Agriculture Survive?*: 376.

izing principle for identifying several distinctive features of agricultural development and the irrigation syndrome in contemporary Japan.

According to the literature analyzed in this research project, Japanese land improvement projects, *tochi kairyō jigyō*, are: heavily dependent on engineering technology, highly intensive in their use of land and water, and designed to include significant monetary subsidies.[2] The illustrations composed for this project serve as a departure point for briefly summarizing these attributes, specifically those composite sketches that deal with the process of farmland consolidation, *hojō seibi*, figure 1, and the premodern and modern patterns of land and water use in wet-paddy areas, figures 2 and 3. In each of these sketches the application of engineering technology results in a remarkable transformation of the agricultural landscape, one that permits a considerably greater degree of water control and land management in each individual field.[3] Such fine-tuning at the site level appears to affect all facets of wet-paddy or dry-field production, including: water supply, distribution, and drainage; the mechanization of a formerly labor-intensive cultivation system; greater protection from natural catastrophes (particularly flood-related); and improvement of the transportation system connecting field, village, and market. Although the composition of these illustrations focuses primarily on the application of engineering technology, each also portrays the degree and intensity of land and water use. Furthermore, the sketches suggest the need for significant amounts of monetary subsidy or cost-sharing based on the sophisticated facilities that are being constructed.

These observations call attention to component parts of an important theme around which contemporary Japanese agriculture might be studied. The illustrations suggest, in short, that one of the major objectives of post-World War II agricultural policy in Japan has been development of a comprehensive approach for both elevating the degree of water control and rationalizing land use at the site level. Of particular importance to an evaluation of the performance of such policy is to assess the functions of LIDs, *Tochi Kairyō Ku*, those organizations that play an essential role in site-level investment in and maintenance of the infrastructure for agricultural production. In chapters 2 through 4 a preliminary attempt was made to analyze the distinguishing features of these districts, with regard to: landscape modification; legal status, operating guidelines, and relationship to

---

[2]   These observations represent a modification of an earlier statement, see Latz, *Nihon ni okeru kangai* [Irrigation in Japan]: 3-5.

[3]   Engineering technology, in effect, permits a greater degree of water control and land management in the entire irrigation network, from water source to individual field, as qualified by the findings of this chapter. Additional illustration of this observation may be found in Latz, *Nihon ni okeru kangai* [Irrigation in Japan]: 65-79.

changing government policies for agricultural development; impact on production yield; and regional variations in operation during the course of rapid industrialization in the post-World War II period.[4]

Surprising insights into the functions of LIDs occur when its operation is studied in the context of a rapidly suburbanizing area of the Kantō plain in Saitama prefecture. It is at this point that the concept of land improvement, to promote coordinated development of the land and water components of the agricultural infrastructure, is forced to confront stubborn environmental, social, and economic conditions at the site level, leading to the conclusion that site conditions have a striking impact on the distribution and function of land improvement projects in the prefecture: LIDs for land readjustment, *kukaku seiri*; farmland consolidation, *hojō seibi*; irrigation and drainage canal maintenance, *iji kanri*; and agricultural water-use rationalization, *nōgyō yōsui gōrika*, do not appear to be coordinated in terms of established criteria which clearly define infrastructure investment in the context of a given irrigation network.

In concept, then, the goal of post-World War II land improvement policy has been to promote coordinated agricultural development. In practice, however, the appeal of the LID, the administrative vehicle for implementing land improvement policy, has been its ability to introduce technology that allows a higher degree of water control and land management at the individual field level. These two expectations, while not necessarily mutually exclusive, are at odds with each other in the case of rapid suburbanization, where changes in land use have the effect of compromising the overall functioning of the irrigation network. Thus, in the Minumadai canal in Saitama prefecture no one organization has the authority to rationalize the irrigation network: the Minuma LID, entrusted with responsibility for the main canal, does not have authority over the branch canals; and the northern, predominantly agricultural center of the benefited area, *jueki chiku*, does not have authority over land sales for nonagricultural uses in the southern portions of the canal.

The pattern of infrastructure investment activity in Saitama prefecture is an impressive critique of contemporary land improvement policy in Japan. Although the institutional structure for infrastructure investment

---

[4]   A brief summary of the functions of LIDs follows. The LID assumes primary responsibility for introducing land improvement projects in a given area. Application for establishment must be initiated by local farmers; once in place, the LID acts to solidify farmer consensus and, if necessary, to exert coercive pressures to ensure participation of all farmers who will benefit from the proposed project. The LID is the representative of farmer interests in discussions with higher levels of government and undertakes responsibility for making cost-sharing applications to the Agricultural, Forestry and Fisheries Finance Corporation, *Nōrin Gyogyō Kinyū Kōko*. It is the LID that assumes debt once the loan is extended, as well as responsibility for collecting the beneficiary share to be repaid to the national finance corporation.

was unified by the *Tochi Kairyō Hō*, Land Improvement Law of 1949, it did not lead to functional consolidation of land and water resources in irrigated agricultural areas. The reasons for this have much to do with the promulgation of a series of countervailing policies promoting site level, as distinct from irrigation network level, development in postwar Japan, beginning with the Land Reform, *Nōchi Kaikaku*, including the Agricultural Basic Law, *Nōgyō Kihon Hō*, and the River Law, *Kasen Hō*, and, most recently, promotion of projects for farmland consolidation, *hojō seibi*. In effect, the present-day institutional structure for infrastructure investment is incapable of promoting coordinated development of agricultural resources in Japan because the object of attention has been the component parts of the irrigation network,[5] *not* comprehensive consolidation of the areal unit bounded by the LID. This problem is especially pronounced in suburbanizing regions in Japan. Parenthetically, it should be reiterated that the language of Japanese agriculture, by its very ambiguity, represents an intriguing metaphor for the problems now facing land improvement policymakers in Japan. As noted previously, particularly in chapter 4, the designations *hojō seibi*, farmland consolidation; *kukaku seiri*, land readjustment; and *nōgyō yōsui gōrika*, agricultural water-use rationalization, do not reflect clearly the land improvement activities with which they are engaged; in the case of the latter, technology is used to rationalize water use without altering customary water rights, *kankō suiri ken*. An additional example of terminology in need of careful definition is *jueki chiku*, benefited area; there is confusion in the policy publications of Japan's LIDs regarding the engineering and institutional meanings of this term.

Clarification of the goal and meaning of land improvement policy is expected to become a priority for Japanese agricultural policymakers in the next decade. In the post-World War II period the LID has been extremely successful at introducing technology that has had the effect of elevating agricultural output in Japan.[6] Questions are now being raised, however, regarding further introduction of new civil engineering projects: does the application of such technology promote change, or does it serve tradition? Based on analysis of the Minumadai irrigation canal it would appear there is a powerful inertia to be overcome if customary water rights, *kankō suiri ken*, are to be reallocated. In short, technology cannot be used indefinitely as a substitute for reallocation of *kankō suiri ken* now controlled by agricul-

---

[5] A good example of this point is the emphasis placed on the terminal point of the irrigation network, the development of which symbolizes both the dominant theme of post-World War II land improvement policy, i.e., *kukaku seiri*, land readjustment, and *hojō seibi*, farmland consolidation, as well as the rising political power of the farmer.

[6] As noted by Tsuchiya, *Progress in Japanese Agriculture*, discussed above in chapter 3.

tural interests in irrigation networks managed by Minuma and affiliated LIDs. The source of this conflict is the persistence of legal customs that can be traced back three hundred years to the beginning of the Tokugawa period, customs based fundamentally on political and regional compromises by agricultural water users. More technologically efficient water transfer will not create the necessary political coalitions needed for regional water management in rapidly developing areas like the Kantō Plain. Properly conceived, institutions like the LID can establish the basis for wise future management of water resources. Improperly conceived, there is the risk that such institutions, ostensibly for agricultural water-use rationalization, will in fact operate as resource development organizations that transfer technology for the purpose of preserving traditional water-use practices.[7]

By way of conclusion it should be noted that the future course of LIDs in suburbanizing areas can be expected to follow the pattern identified in the Saitama case. There will be continued parallel but uncoordinated development of those districts concerned ostensibly with land readjustment, kukaku seiri, or farmland consolidation, hojō seibi, and those concerned with irrigation and drainage canal maintenance, iji kanri, as well as projects for agricultural water-use rationalization, nōgyō yōsui gōrika. In the case of the latter it is anticipated that there will be an increasing tendency for the role of the LID to change from promotion of agricultural development to that of assuming responsibility for representing the farmer's customary water rights, kankō suiri ken, in negotiations with other organizations calling for reduction in agricultural water use. This shift, from a production goal to one that maintains the customary social fabric of an agricultural area, represents a significant change in the function of LIDs, and also suggests that this political administrative unit is now acting as an impediment to regional development in Japan.[8]

---

[7] Japanese scholars interviewed by the author were generally skeptical about the proposition that LIDs promote comprehensive change in agricultural areas, noting that in terms of agricultural water-use it is tradition, not technology, that may explain contemporary circumstances. This view contrasts with the findings of Shimpo, *Three Decades in Shiwa*, 1976, chapter 1, especially pp. 21-23, which concludes that the introduction of technology is a major force for change in irrigation practices. My observations may also be contrasted to Kornhauser's review of Kelly's *Water Control in Tokugawa Japan*, and his concern that traditional agricultural water use has little to do with contemporary water management problems in Japan's commercial and industrial centers; customary irrigation practices appear to play a key role in regional water management prospects in the case of the Minumadai canal.

[8] This key point is missing from Kelly's otherwise cogent review of Japanese social science research on irrigation; see Kelly, *Irrigation Management in Japan*: 39-59. It is also missing from the work of Tamaki Akira, *Tochi kairyō ku to buraku* [The Land Improvement District and the Village], Nōson Soshiki Kenkyū no Shirīzu, no. 5 (Tokyo: Nōson Chūō Kinkō Kenkyū Sentā, 1976). This paper has already offered a basic disagreement with Kelly regarding definition of the LID as essentially an irrigation grouping. A second example of the shift in

The future prospect of the LID is not necessarily determined by the Saitama findings, however. The challenge facing land improvement policy-makers in Japan is to devise an institutional structure that is appropriate for a variety of regional circumstances in the country. In the case of rapidly suburbanizing areas, it will be necessary to balance regional needs for non-agricultural water use and maintenance of the canal function in a clearly definable irrigation network and its corresponding benefited area, *jueki chiku*. This balance may include granting powers to the district, which would restrict farmers from freely selling land. At the same time, policy-makers should consider alternative institutional structures for promoting agricultural production in those regions where suburbanization is not occurring.

It is interesting to note that the need to devise an institutional structure appropriate to diverse agricultural regions in Japan is far different from the prevailing recommendations in the Japanese and American engin-eering literature, which increasingly seem to overemphasize data collection for long-range planning purposes. Changing land-use patterns in the area within and adjacent to an irrigation network can indeed be analyzed objec-tively and confirm the nature of the site-level problem, but such data cannot substitute for essential political compromise between landowners and water users in rapidly suburbanizing areas.[9] Instead, one may predict that com-petition over relatively fixed amounts of water and land will increase in Japan's larger metropolitan regions, to be resolved in the midst of a crisis related to water demand and supply, by reallocating *kankō suiri ken*, agricultural water rights. The transformation of the agricultural landscape into an urban-industrial landscape, which appears to have been the major preoccupation of the Japanese since the turn of the century, will not be complete until water resources are so defined.

LID function to maintenance of the customary (rural) social fabric is that by 1979 the menu of possible land improvement projects totaled over 400, only eighty of which are primarily related to the major objectives of LIDs.

[9] Field work between 1980 and 1983 indicated that in the Saitama case little effort is made to distinguish between the category of land use, i.e., *suiden*, wet-paddy fields, or *hatake nōgyō*, dry-field agriculture, and actual land use in the prefecture. In effect, agricultural officials have no clear-cut idea of the exact location or nature of water demand throughout the Minumadai irrigation canal. In addition, there is little coordinated data collection by the Arable Land Department and the Urban Land Planning Department at the Saitama Prefectural Office. Even so, if such coordination were to occur, and if the United States is an example, heavy emphasis on data collection has led to only limited accomplishments in the field of river basin planning. I would like to acknowledge James Wescoat, Jr., University of Chicago, for the latter observation.

APPENDIX: GLOSSARY

ア

アール *āru,* are
暗渠排水 *ankyo haisui,* underdrainage

イ

維持管理 *iji kanri,* irrigation and drainage canal maintenance

オ

温水池 *onsui ike,* water warming pond
温水施設 *onsui shisetsu,* water warming facilities
温水路 *onsui ro,* water warming canal

カ

開墾 *kaikon,* land reclamation
開拓 *kaitaku,* land reclamation
掛流し *kake nagashi,* plot-to-plot irrigation
河川法 *Kasen Hō,* River Law
可動堰 *kadō zeki,* movable weir
瓦葺 *Kawarabuki*
灌漑 *kangai,* irrigation
灌漑排水 *kangai haisui,* irrigation and drainage
慣行水利権 *kankō suiri ken,* customary water right
幹線排水路 *kansen haisui ro,* drainage canal, main
幹線用水路 *kansen yōsui ro,* irrigation canal, main (trunk)
関東流 *Kantō ryū,* Kantō River training method

キ

緊急開拓事業　*kinkyū kaitaku jigyō,* emergency land reclamation
project

ク

区　*ku,* ward
区画整理　*kukaku seiri,* land readjustment

ケ

京浜　*Keihin*
決済金　*kessai kin,* liquidation levy
県営事業　*kenei jigyō,* prefecture-operated project
兼業農家　*kengyō nōka,* part-time farm household
減水深　*gensuishin,* water depth requirement
県単　*kentan,* see 県単独事業
県単独事業　*kentandoku jigyō,* independent prefecture-operated
project

コ

交換分合　*kokan bungō,* land exchange and consolidation
耕地整備　*kōchi seibi,* land improvement (special academic usage)
耕地整理　*kōchi seiri,* arable land reorganization
耕地整理組合　*Kōchi Seiri Kumiai,* Arable Land Reorganization
Association
耕地整理法　*Kōchi Seiri Hō,* Arable Land Reorganization Law
国営事業　*kokuei jigyō,* government-operated project
固定堰　*kotei zeki,* fixed weir

サ

災害復旧　*saigai fukyū,* damaged land rehabilitation
最小用水路　*saishō yōsui ro,* ditch (sub-branch) canal

シ

市　*shi,* city
支線排水路　*shisen haisui ro,* branch (sub-main) drainage canal

支線用水路　*shisen yōsui ro,*　branch (sub-main) irrigation canal
自然流下型取水施設　*shizen ryuka gata shusui shisetsu,* gravity-type
　　　irrigation intake facilities
市町村　*shichōson,*　city, town and village (settlement pattern)
柴山　*Shibayama*
集水渠　*shusui kyo,*　collecting drain
受益地区　*jueki chiku,*　benefited area
熟地　*jukuchi,*　land ripening
取水堰　*shusui zeki,*　diversion weir
小排水路　*shohaisui ro,*　lateral drainage canal
食料管理制度　*shokuryō kanri seido,*　staple foodstuff control system
諸土地改良　*sho tochi kairyō,*　other types of land improvement
代掻き　*shirokaki,*　surface soil puddling

ス

水田　*suiden,*　wet-paddy field
水田農業　*suiden nōgyō,*　wet-paddy agriculture, wet-field agriculture
水利慣行　*suiri kankō,*　customary water-use practices
水利組合条例　*Suiri Kumiai Jōrei,*　Ordinance for Water-Use
　　　Associations

セ

生産調整　*seisan chōsei,*　production adjustment
制度金融　*seido kinyū,*　institutional financing
堰　*seki,*　weir (can also refer to dams, headworks, canals, and irrigation
　　　network)
専業農家　*sengyō nōka,*　full-time farm household

ソ

村　*son,*　village

タ

第一種兼業農家　*dai isshu kengyō nōka,*　type-1 part-time farm
　　　household (mainly engaged in farming)
第二種兼業農家　*dai nishu kengyō nōka,*　type-2 part-time farm
　　　household (mainly engaged in other jobs)
田越し灌漑　*tagoshi kangai,*　plot-to-plot irrigation
溜池　*tameike,*　pond/small reservoir

団体営事業　*dantaiei jigyō,*　organization-operated project

チ

地下排水網　*chika haisui mō,*　underdrainage network
町　*chō,*　town

ツ

通船堀　*tsūsen bori,*　canal, transport-type

テ

田区改正　*denku kaisei,*　farm lot adjustment

ト

頭首工　*tōshukō,*　headworks
徳川　*Tokugawa*
土地改良　*tochi kairyō,*　land improvement
土地改良区　*Tochi Kairyō Ku,*　Land Improvement District
土地改良事業　*tochi kairyō jigyō,*　land improvement project
土地改良政策　*tochi kairyō seisaku,*　land improvement policy
土地改良法　*Tochi Kairyō Hō,*　Land Improvement Law
土地改良施設維持管理　*tochi kairyō shisetsu iji kanri,*　land
　　　improvement facilities for maintenance control
利根大堰　*Tone ōzeki,*　Tone headworks　(large-scale)

ナ

中干し　*nakaboshi,*　mid-summer drainage
斜め堰　*naname zeki,*　slanted weir

ノ

農業基盤整備　*nōgyō kiban seibi,*　agricultural infrastructure
　　　consolidation
農業基本法　*Nōgyō Kihon Hō,*　Agricultural Basic Law
農業協同組合（農協）　*Nōgyō Kyōdō Kumiai (Nokyo),*
　　　Agricultural Cooperative Association
（農業協同）組合金融　*(Nōgyō Kyōdō) Kumiai Kinyū,*　(Agricultural
　　　Cooperative) Association Financing

農業構造改善　*nōgyō kōzō kaizen*,　agricultural structure improvement
農業構造改善事業　*nōgyō kōzō kaizen jigyō*,　agricultural structure improvement project
農業用水合理化　*nōgyō yōsui gōrika*,　agricultural water-use rationalization
農業用水合理化事業　*nōgyō yōsui gōrika jigyō*,　agricultural water-use rationalization project
農村整備　*nōson seibi*,　village consolidation
農村総合整備　*nōson sōgō seibi*,　comprehensive village consolidation
農地改革　*nōchi kaikaku*,　land reform
農地整備　*nōchi seibi*,　agricultural land consolidation
農地造成　*nōchi zōsei*,　land reclamation
農地法　*Nōchi Hō*,　Agricultural Land Law
農地防災保全　*nōchi bōsai hozen*,　project for protection of agricultural lands susceptible to natural disasters
農道整備　*nōdō seibi*,　farm road consolidation
農用地開発　*nōyōchi kaihatsu*,　agricultural land development
農林漁業金融公庫　*Nōrin Gyogyō Kinyū Kōko*,　Agriculture, Forestry and Fisheries Finance Corporation
農林水産省（農林省）*Nōrinsuisanshō (Nōrinshō)*,　Ministry of Agriculture, Forestry and Fisheries
農林部　*Nōrinbu*,　Agricultural Department

ハ

梅雨　*baiu*,　early summer rainy season (plum rains)
排水弁　*haisui ben*,　relief well, (modern)
排水路　*haisui ro*,　drainage canal, (modern)
幕府　*bakufu*,　feudal government
畑　*hatake*,　dry field
畑地帯総合土地改良　*hatake chitai sōgō tochi kairyō*,　comprehensive land improvement of dry-field zones
畑農業　*hatake nōgyō*,　dry-field agriculture
八郎潟　*Hachirōgata*

ヒ

非補助事業　*hihojo jigyō*,　unsubsidized project
標準区画　*hyōjun kukaku*,　standard farmland block

フ

吹出し口　*fuki dashi guchi,*　spigot-type water valve
普通水利組合　*Futsū Suiri Kumiai,*　Regular Water-Use Association
普通水利組合法　*Futsū Suiri Kumiai Hō,*　Regular Water-Use
　　Association Law

ヘ

米穀法　*Beikoku Hō,*　Rice Law

ホ

圃場整備　*hojō seibi,*　farmland consolidation
圃場整備事業　*hojō seibi jigyō,*　farmland consolidation project
補助金　*hojokin,*　subsidies
補助残融資　*hojo zan yūshi,*　financing for the nonsubsidized portion

マ

町　*machi,*　town
回し水路　*mawashi suiro,*　detour canal

ミ

水資源開発公団　*Mizu Shigen Kaihatsu Kōdan,*　Water Resources
　　Development Public Corporation
水資源開発促進法　*Mizu Shigen Kaihatsu Sokushin Hō,*　Water
　　Resources Development Promotion Law
見沼台　*Minumadai*

ム

武蔵水路　*Musashi suiro,*　Musashi canal

メ

名簿　*meibo,*　register of district names

ヨ

用水路　*yōsui ro,* irrigation canal (modern)
用排水改良事業補助要項　*Yōhaisui Kairyō Jigyō Hojō Yōkō,*
Rules for Subsidization of Irrigation and Drainage Projects
用排水幹線改良　*yōhaisui kansen kairyō,* mainline irrigation and
drainage canal improvement
用排水施設　*yōhaisui shisetsu,* irrigation and drainage facilities

レ

連続灌漑　*renzoku kangai,* continuous irrigation

BIBLIOGRAPHY

Books and Monographs in Japanese

Asami Yoshiichi et al. *Nōgyō hyakka jiten, taikei* [Encyclopedia of Agri-culture, Comprehensive Edition]. Tokyo: Nōsei Chōsa Iinkai, 1966. 8 vols.

Hanayama Yuzuru. *Toshi to mizushigen--mizu no seiji keizai gaku* [Cities and Water Resources--The Political Economy of Water]. Tokyo: Ka-shima Publishing Co., 1977.

Imamura Naraomi. *Hojokin to nōgyō, nōson* [Villages, Agriculture, and Subsidies]. Tokyo: Ie no Hikari Kyōkai, 1982.

Imamura Naraomi et al. *Tochi kairyō hyaku nen shi* [A Hundred Years of Land Improvement]. Tokyo: Heibonsha, 1977.

Ishibashi Yutaka et al. *Nōgyō suiri gaku* [Agricultural Water Use]. Tokyo: Asakura Shoten, 1977.

Isozaki Hisashi, ed. *Kangai haisui* [Irrigation and Drainage]. Tokyo: Yō-kendō Co., 1978.

Japan Times, ed. *Shuyōkoku gyōsei kikō handobukku* [Administrative Organizations Handbook for Principal Countries]. Tokyo: Japan Times, 1980.

Jurisuto Sōgō Tokushū, ed. *Gendai no mizu mondai, kadai to tenbō* [Contemporary Problems of Water Resources, Tasks and Perspec-tives]. Summer, no. 23, Tokyo: Yūhikaku, July 1981.

Kaneko Ryō, ed. *N ōgyō suimon gaku* [Agricultural Hydrology]. Tokyo: Kyōritsu Publishing Co., 1978.

Kensetsushō Kokudochiribu, ed. *Nihon kokusei chizuchō* [The National Atlas of Japan]. Tokyo: Nihon Chizu Sentā, 1978.

Latz, Gil. *Nihon ni okeru kangai ni kan suru waei yōgo shū fuzuhyō* [Contemporary and Historical Irrigation in Japan--Selected Terminology and Illustrations]. Tokyo: Toyota Foundation, 1986.

Minumadai Tochi Kairyō Ku. *Minumadai yōsuiro tochi kairyō ku iji kanri keikakusho* [Planning Documents for Irrigation and Drainage Maintenance of the Minumadai Irrigation Canal]. Urawa: Minumadai Tochi Kairyō Ku, 1953.

Minuma Tochi Kairyō Ku. *Minuma tochi kairyō ku kakunen no sōdaikai gian* [Annual Representative Sessions of the Minuma Land Improvement District]. Urawa: Minuma Tochi Kairyō Ku, annual since 1953.

_____. *Tsūjō sōdaikai gian* [Regular Representative Sessions]. Urawa: Minuma Tochi Kairyō Ku, annual 1953-80.

_____. *Minumadai yōsui kaihatsu 250 nen kinen--shiori* [The 250th Anniversary of the Development of the Minumadai Irrigation Canal--Handbook]. Urawa: Minuma Tochi Kairyō Ku, 1977.

_____. *Minuma tochi kairyō ku teikan* [Minuma Land Improvement District Articles of Incorporation]. Urawa: Minuma Tochi Kairyō Ku, n.d.

Miyama Heihachiro et al. *N ōgaku yōgo shū* [A Glossary of (English, Japanese, and Vietnamese) Agricultural Terms]. Tokyo: Saikon Publishing Co., 1975.

Moritaki Kenichirō. *Gendai no mizu shigen mondai* [Contemporary Water Resource Problems]. Tokyo: Chōbunsha, 1982.

Nihon, Sorifu Tōkeikyoku. *Shōwa 55 nen kokusei chōsa hōkoku ken betsu waga kuni no jinkō shūchū chiku* [Concentrated Population Districts of the Nation, 1980]. Tokyo: Nihon Tōkei Kyōkai, 1983.

_____. *Showa 35 nen kokusei chōsa hōkoku ken betsu waga kuni no jinkō shūchū chiku* [Concentrated Population Districts of the Nation, 1960]. Tokyo: Nihon Tōkei Kyōkai, 1962.

Nōgyō Doboku Gakkai. *Nōgyō doboku hyōjun yōgo jiten, kaiteiban* [Dictionary of Standard Terms for Agricultural Engineering, rev. ed.]. Tokyo: Nōgyō Doboku Gakkai, 1974.

Nōgyō Suiri Kenkyūkai, ed. *Nihon no nōgyō yōsui* [Agricultural Water Use in Japan]. Tokyo: Chikusha, 1980.

Nōrinsuisanshō. *Nōgyō hakusho fuzoku tōkeihyō* (annual) [Agricultural White Paper on Statistical Matters]. Tokyo: Nōrinsuisanshō, 1981.

Nōrinsuisanshō Keizaikyoku Tōkeijōhōbu, ed. *Poketto nōrin suisan tōkei, 1983* [Agriculture, Forestry and Fisheries Statistics, 1983 Pocket Edition]. Tokyo: Nōrin Tōkeikyokai, 1983 (published annually).

Nōrinsuisanshō Kōchika. *Nōchi to kaihō jisseki chōsa* [Survey Results of the Agricultural Land Reform]. Tokyo: Nōrinsuisanshō, 1956.

Nōrinsuisanshō Kōzōkaizenkyoku. *Tochi kairyō jigyō keikaku sekkei kijun--ankyo haisui* [Standard Design Plans for Land Improvement Projects--Field Underdrainage]. Tokyo: Nōrinsuisanshō Kōzōkaizenkyoku, 1979.

_____. *Tochi kairyō jigyō keikaku sekkei kijun--haisui* [Standard Design Plans for Land Improvement Projects--Drainage]. Tokyo: Nōrinsuisanshō Kōzōkaizenkyoku, 1979.

_____. *Tochi kairyō jigyō keikaku sekkei kijun--hojō seibi (hatake)* [Standard Design Plans for Land Improvement Projects--Farmland Consolidation (Dry Field)]. Tokyo: Nōrinsuisanshō Kōzōkaizenkyoku, 1979.

_____. *Tochi kairyō jigyō keikaku sekkei kijun--hojō seibi (suiden)* [Standard Design Plans for Land Improvement Projects--Farmland Consolidation (Wet-Paddy Field)]. Tokyo: Nōrinsuisanshō Kōzōkaizenkyoku, 1977.

_____. *Tochi kairyō jigyō keikaku sekkei kijun--nōchi hozen* [Standard Design Plans for Land Improvement Projects--Agricultural Land Protection]. Tokyo: Nōrinsuisanshō Kōzōkaizenkyoku, 1979.

_____. *Tochi kairyō jigyō keikaku sekkei kijun--nōchi kaihatsu (kaibatake)* [Standard Design Plans for Land Improvement Projects--Farmland Development (Dry Field)]. Tokyo: Nōrinsuisanshō Kōzōkaizenkyoku, 1977.

_____. *Tochi kairyō jigyō keikaku sekkei kijun--nōdō* [Standard Design Plans for Land Improvement--Agricultural Roads]. Tokyo: Nōrinsuisanshō Kōzōkaizenkyoku, 1981.

Nōrinsuisanshō Kōzōkaizenkyoku, ed. *Tochi kairyō ho kaisetsu* [Land Improvement Law Commentary]. Rev. ed. Tokyo: Zenkoku Tochi Kairyō Jigyō Dantai Rengō Kai, 1974.

Nōrinsuisanshō Kōzōkaizenkyoku Kensetsubu, ed. *Tochi kairyō no zenyō* [Comprehensive Summary of Land Improvement]. Tokyo: Kōkyōjigyō Tsūshinsha, 1979.

_____. *Tochi kairyō no zenyō--kaisetsu to shiryō* [Comprehensive Summary of Land Improvement–Explanation and Data]. Tokyo: Kōkyōjigyō Tsūshinsha, 1979.

_____. *Tochi kairyō no zenyō--kaisetsu to shiryō* [Comprehensive Summary of Land Improvement--Explanation and Data]. Tokyo: Kōkyōjigyō Tsūshinsha, 1982.

Nōrinsuisanshō Kōzōkaizenkyoku Kensetsubu Sekkeika, ed. *Tochi kairyō yōran* [Summary of Land Improvement]. Tokyo: Nōrinsuisanshō Kōzōkaizenkyoku Kensetsubu Sekkeika, 1981.

Nōsei Chōsa Iinkai, ed. *Nōson chiiki shigen* [Rural Regional Resources]. Nihon no nōgyō--asu e no ayumi 132 (December 1980).

Ogata Hiroyuki, ed. *Mizu to nihon nōgyō* [Water and Japanese Agriculture]. Tokyo: Tokyo Daigaku Shuppan Kai, 1979.

Okabe Saburō. *Zusetsu tochi kairyō 100 kō--asu no nōson kensetsu o mezashite* (One Hundred Lectures on Land Improvement--Toward Future Rural Development]. Tokyo: Chikusha, 1979.

Ōtani Seizo, ed. *Tochi kairyō o kangaeru* [Thoughts about Land Improvement]. Tokyo: Japan Irrigation Club, 1978.

Saitama Ken. *Saitama ken no tochi kairyō (jigyō gaiyō)* [Land Improvement in Saitama Prefecture (Project Summary)]. Urawa: Saitama Ken, 1981.

_____. *Saitama ken no tochi kairyō (jigyō gaiyō)* [Land Improvement in Saitama Prefecture (Project Summary)]. Urawa: Saitama Ken, 1983.

Saitama Ken Nōrinbu. *Saitama no nōrinsuisangyō* [Agriculture, Forestry and Fishery Production in Saitama]. Urawa: Saitama Ken, 1981.

_____. *Saitama nō norinsuisangyō* [Agriculture, Forestry and Fishery Production in Saitama]. Urawa: Saitama Ken, 1983.

Saitama Ken Nōrinbu Kōchikeikakuka. *Showa 57 shigatsu tsuitachi genzai tochi kairyō ku meibo* [April 1, 1982, Register of Land Improvement Districts]. Urawa: Saitama Ken, 1982.

Saitama Ken Tochi Kairyō Jigyō Dantai Rengō Kai, ed. *Saitama no tochi kairyō* [Land Improvement in Saitama]. Urawa: Saitama Ken Tochi Kairyō Jigyō Dantai Rengō Kai, 1977.

Shimura Hiroyasu. *Gendai suiri ron* [A Study of Modern Water Use]. Tokyo: Tokyo Daigaku Shuppan Kai, 1982.

Shinzawa Kagato. *Nōgyō suiri ron* [A Study of Irrigation]. Tokyo: Tokyo Daigaku Shuppan Kai, 1955. Reissued 1980.

_____. *Tochi kairyō ron* [A Study of Land Improvement]. Tokyo: Tokyo Daigaku Shuppan Kai, 1955.

Shirai Yoshihiko. *Nihon no kōchi seibi* [Land Improvement in Japan]. Tokyo: Taimeidō, 1972.

Suiri Kagaku Kenkyūjo, ed. *Suimon yōgo shū* [Compilation of Hydrological Terms]. Tokyo: Suiri Kagaku Kenkyūjo, 1975.

Suzuki Motosuke. *Jitsuyō nōgyō eigo shōjiten* [Practical English Dictionary of Agriculture]. Tokyo: Nōgyōtosho Co., 1978.

Tamaki Akira. *Tochi kairyō ku to buraku* [The Land Improvement District and the Village]. Nōson Soshiki Kenkyū no Shīrizu, no. 5. Tokyo: Nōson Chūō Kinkō Kenkyū Sentā, 1976.

Tamaki Akira, Hatate Isao, and Imamura Naraomi. *Suiri no shakai kōzō* [The Social Structure of Water Use]. Tokyo: Tokyo Daigaku Shuppan Kai, 1984.

Yamazaki Fujio. *Nōchi kōgaku* [Agricultural Land Civil Engineering]. Tokyo: Tokyo Daigaku Shuppan Kai, 1977. 2 vols.

Zenkoku Tochi Kairyō Jigyō Dantai Rengō Kai, ed. *Nōgyō kiban seibi jigyō no shakaiteki yakuwari* [The Social Function of Agricultural Infrastructure Consolidation]. Tokyo: Zenkoku Tochi Kairyō Dantai Rengō Kai, 1981.

Articles in Japanese

Mizutani Masakazu. "Toshika to nōgyō yōsui" [Urbanization and Agricultural Water Use]. In *Mizu to nihon nōgyō* [Water and Japanese Agriculture], edited by Ogata Hiroyuki, pp. 285-305. Tokyo: Tokyo Daigaku Shuppan Kai, 1979.

Moritaki Kenichirō. "Keizai chiri gaku ni okeru suiri mondai kenkyū no kadai to hōhō" [Methods and Topics for Research on Water-Use Problems in the Field of Economic Geography]. *Keizai Chiri Gaku Nenpō* 12, no. 1 (1966): 1-16.

Naga Akira. "Tochi kairyō jigyō to tochi kairyō ku" [Land Improvement Projects and Land Improvement Districts]. *Nōgyō Doboku Gakkai Shi* 47, no. 10 (October 1979): 759-62.

Nishikawa Osamu. "Nihon ni okeru tochi riyō to tochi kairyō ni arawareta chiikiteki tokushoku" [Regional Characteristics of Land Use and Land Improvement in Japan]. *Tokyo Daigaku Kyōyōgaku-bu, Jinbunkagaku-ka Kiyō (Jinbunchiri-gaku)* 34 (1965): 42-61.

_____. "Nihon ni okeru tochi kairyō ku no bumpu" [The Distribution of Land Improvement Districts in Japan]. *Tokyo Daigaku Kyōyōgaku-bu, Jinbunkagaku-ka Kiyō (Jinbunchiri-gaku)* 38 (1966): 17-24.

Shibata Kyohei. "Nōgyō suiri no shisutemu ni kan suru ichi kosatsu--hōseijō no soshiki o chūshin ni" [One Consideration Concerning the Agricultural Water-Use System--Centered on the Organization of the Legal System]. *Tokyo Daigaku Kyōyōgaku-bu, Jinbunkagaku-ka Kiyō (Jinbunchiri-gaku 8)* 78 (March 1983): 65-89.

_____. "Daitoshi kinkō ni okeru nōgyō suiri soshiki no henyō--Saitama ken minuma tochi kairyō ku no baii" [Evolution and Response of Agricultural Water-Use Organizations to Suburbanization and Demand for Water Rationalization--The Case of the Minuma Land Improvement District]. *Chigaku Zasshi* 94, no. 1 (1985): 1-20.

Shimura Hiroyasu. "Minumadai yōsui" [Minumadai Irrigation Canal]. *Nihon no Kagaku to Gijutsu* '79/Maikurokonputa: 90-96.

Shirai Yoshihiko. "Nihon ni okeru nōchi shūdanka chiiki no shosō" [Some Phases of Regional Farmland Consolidation in Japan]. *Chirigaku Hyōron* 37 (1964): 425-29.

Tabayashi Akira. "Hokuriku chihō ni okeru nōgyō suiri no kukan kōzō" [Spatial Structure of Irrigation Systems in Hokuriku District]. *Chirigaku Hyōron* 54, no. 6 (June 1981): 295-316.

_____. "Hokuriku chihō ni okeru nōgyō suiri no kukan kōzō no keisei katei" [Formation of the Spatial Structure of Irrigation Systems in Hokuriku District]. *Tsukuba Daigaku, Chikyū-ka Gaku-kei, (Jinbunchirigaku kenkyushitsu)* 6 (March 1983): 1-28.

Pamphlets and Maps in Japanese.

Ina Yoshihiko. "Minumadai yōsui no oitachi" [The Historical Background
    of the Minumadai Irrigation Canal]. 1982.

Minuma Tochi Kairyō Ku. "Minuma tochi kairyō ku iji kanri keikakusho
    fuzu" [Planning Documents and Illustrations for Maintenance Con-
    trol in the Minuma Land Improvement District]. 1:50,000. n.d.

Mizushigen Kaihatsu Kōdan. "Tone dōsui jigyō gaiyō" [Summary Descrip-
    tion of the Tone River Water Conveyance Project]. Tokyo: Mizu-
    shigen Kaihatsu Kōdan, 1979.

_____. "Saitama goguchi nikki jigyō keikaku no gaiyō" [Summary Project
    Plan for Unification in Saitama]. 1981. Pamphlet.

Saitama Ken. "Saitama goguchi nikki jigyō zentai keikaku (gaiyō)" [Com-
    plete Plans for Stage Two Unification Projects in Saitama (Sum-
    mary)]. Urawa: Saitama Ken, n.d.

_____. "Ōmiya tochi kairyō jimusho kannai tochi kairyō ku kuiki zu"
    [Regional Map of Land Improvement Districts under the Jurisdiction
    of the Ōmiya Land Improvement Office]. 1:50,000. n.d.

Saitama Ken Nōrinbu Kōchijigyōka. "Nōchi seibi (kukaku seiri) kanryō-
    chiku chōsahyō" [Data on Completed Areas of Agricultural Land
    Consolidation (Land Readjustment)]. Urawa: Saitama Ken, n.d.

Saitama Ken Ōmiya Tochi Kairyō Jimusho. "Saitama goguchi nikki jigyō
    keikaku ippan zu" [General Plan for Stage Two Unification Projects].
    1:75,000. 1981.

_____. "Saitama goguchi nikki jigyō keikaku gaiyō" [Summary Plan for Uni-
    fication Projects in Saitama]. 1981.

Zenkoku Tochi Kairyō Jigyō Dantai Rengō Kai, ed. "Nōgyō kiban no seibi"
    [Consolidation of the Agricultural Infrastructure]. Tokyo: Zenkoku
    Tochi Kairyō Jigyō Dantai Rengō Kai, 1982.

Unpublished Sources in Japanese

Latz, Gil. "'Nihon to amerika ni okeru nōgyō mizu shigen seisaku no rinen to jissai no hikaku kenkyū' ni kan suru yobiteki kenkyū" [Preparatory Research for a Comparison of Agricultural Water Resource Management Policy Concepts and Practice in Japan and the United States]. Report to the Toyota Foundation, 1981-82, grant 80-1-192.

Saitama Ken. Archival materials regarding maintenance plans for Land Improvement Districts in Saitama Prefecture, n.d.

Shibata Kyōhei. "Saitama ken minumadai yōsui ni okeru nōgyō suiri shisutemu--toshika e no taiō o chūshin ni" [Agricultural Water-Use System in Minumadai Canal of Saitama Prefecture--Centering on the Impact of Urbanization]. Manuscript, March 1984.

Tokyo Daigaku, Jinbunchiri Kenkyūshitsu. "Nihon ni okeru tochi kairyō ku no bumbu" [The Distribution of Land Improvement Districts in Japan]. Tokyo: Tokyo Daigaku Jinbuchiri Kenkyūshitsu, Spring 1982.

Books and Monographs in English

Ackerman, Edward A. *Japan's Natural Resources and Their Relation to Japan's Economic Future*. Chicago: University of Chicago Press, 1953.

Association of Japanese Geographers, ed. *Geography of Japan*. Tokyo: Special Publication no. 4, Teikoku-Shoin Co., 1980.

Beardsley, Richard K.; Hall, John W.; and Ward, Robert E. *Village Japan*. Chicago: University of Chicago Press, 1959.

Cantor, Leonard. *A World Geography of Irrigation*. London: Oliver and Boyd, 1967.

Castle, Emery N., and Hemmi, Kenzō. *U.S.-Japanese Agricultural Trade Relations*. Baltimore: Johns Hopkins University Press, 1982.

Coward, E. Walter, Jr., ed. *Irrigation and Agricultural Development in Asia*. Ithaca: Cornell University Press, 1981.

Dempster, Prue. *Japan Advances: A Geographical Study.* London: Methuen, 1969.

Dore, Ronald P. *Land Reform in Japan.* London: Oxford University Press, 1959.

_____. *Shinohata: A Portrait of a Japanese Village.* New York: Pantheon, 1978.

Ebato Akira. *Postwar Japanese Agriculture.* Tokyo: International Society for Educational Information Press, 1973.

Foreign Press Center/Japan. *Facts and Figures of Japan.* Tokyo: Foreign Press Center/Japan, 1980.

Francks, Penelope. *Technology and Agricultural Development in Pre-War Japan.* New Haven, Conn.: Yale University Press, 1983.

Fukutake Tadashi. *Japanese Rural Society.* Translated by Ronald P. Dore. Ithaca, N.Y.: Cornell University Press, 1972.

_____. *Rural Society in Japan.* Tokyo: University of Tokyo Press, 1980.

Geertz, Clifford. *Agricultural Involution: The Process of Ecological Change in Indonesia.* Berkeley: University of California Press, 1963.

Ginsburg, Norton, ed. *The Pattern of Asia.* Inglewood Cliffs, N. J.: Prentice-Hall, 1958.

Grist, D. H. *Rice.* London: Longman, 1959.

Hall, Robert B., Jr. *Japan: Industrial Power of Asia.* 2d ed. New York: D. Van Nostrand Co., 1976.

Hayami Yūjirō. *A Century of Agricultural Growth in Japan.* Tokyo: University of Tokyo Press, 1975.

Ishikawa Shigeru. *Economic Development in Asian Perspective.* Tokyo: Kinokuniya Bookstore Co., 1967.

Itasaka Gen, ed. *Encyclopedia of Japan.* 8 vols. Tokyo: Kodansha Publishing Co., 1983.

Japan. *The Agriculture Basic Law of 1961*. Tokyo: Ministry of Agriculture and Forestry, Law no. 127, 1961.

_____. *Abstract of Statistics on Agriculture, Forestry, and Fisheries*. Tokyo: Ministry of Agriculture, Forestry and Fisheries, 1975.

_____. *The Third Comprehensive National Development Plan*. Tokyo: National Land Agency of Japan, 1979.

_____. *Statistical Handbook of Japan, 1980*. Tokyo: Bureau of Statistics, Prime Minister's Office, 1980.

Japan, Administrative Management Agency. *Organization of the Government of Japan*. Tokyo: Prime Minister's Office, 1983 (published annually).

Japan Economic Research Center, ed. *Agriculture and Economic Development--Structural Readjustment in Asian Perspective*. 2 vols. Tokyo: Japan Economic Research Center, 1972.

Japan Food and Agricultural Organization. *Integrated Rural Development in Japan*. Tokyo: Japan Food and Agricultural Organization, 1976.

_____. *What Will Be the Agricultural Policies of Japan in the 1980s?* Tokyo: Japan Food and Agricultural Organization, 1982.

Japan, Ministry of Agriculture, Forestry and Fisheries, Statistics and Information Department. *Crop Statistics* (annual). Tokyo: Ministry of Agriculture, Forestry and Fisheries, 1982.

Japan, Ministry of Agriculture, Forestry and Fisheries, Statistics and Information Department, ed. *Abstract of Statistics on Agriculture, Forestry and Fisheries: Japan/1982*. Tokyo: Association of Agriculture, Forestry and Fishery Statistics, 1983.

Japan Rural Development Planning Commission. *Rural Development and Planning in Japan*. Tokyo: Rural Development Planning Commission, 1981.

Japanese Society of Irrigation, Drainage, and Reclamation Engineering, International Affairs Commission, ed. *Irrigation and Drainage in*

Japan. Tokyo: Japanese Society of Irrigation, Drainage, and Reclamation Engineering, 1972.

_____, ed. *Irrigation and Drainage in Japan Pictorial*. Tokyo: Japanese Society of Irrigation, Drainage, and Reclamation Engineering, 1978.

Kelly, William W *Irrigation Management in Japan: A Critical Review of Japanese Social Science Research*. Ithaca, N.Y.: Cornell University East Asia Papers, no. 30, 1982.

_____. *Water Control in Tokugawa Japan: Irrigation Organization in a Japanese River Basin, 1600-1870*. Ithaca, N.Y.: Cornell University East Asia Papers, no. 31, 1982.

Kiuchi Shinzo, ed. *Geography in Japan*. Tokyo: University of Tokyo Press, Special Publication no. 3, Association of Japanese Geographers, 1976.

Kornhauser, David. *Japan: Geographical Background to Urban-Industrial Development*. 2d ed. London: Longman Group, 1982.

Latz, Gil. *Contemporary and Historical Irrigation in Japan: Selected Terminology and Illustrations* [Nihon ni okeru kangai ni kan suru waei yōgō shū fuzuhyō]. Tokyo: Toyota Foundation, 1986.

Lockwood, William. *The State and Economic Enterprise in Japan*. Princeton: Princeton University Press, 1968.

Matsuo, Takane. *Rice and Rice Cultivation in Japan*. Tokyo: Institute of Asian Economic Affairs, 1961.

Moore, Richard H. *Japanese Agriculture: Patterns of Rural Development* (Boulder: Westview, in press).

Nakamura, James I. *Agricultural Production and Economic Development of Japan, 1873 to 1922*. Princeton: Princeton University Press, 1966.

Ogura Takekazu. *Can Japanese Agriculture Survive?* 2d ed. Tokyo: Agricultural Policy Research Center, 1980.

_____, ed. *Agricultural Development in Modern Japan*. Tokyo: Fuji Publishing Co., 1967.

Ohkawa, K.; Johnston, Bruce; and Kaneda, H. *Agriculture and Economic Growth--Japan's Experience*. Tokyo: University of Tokyo Press, 1969.

Organization for Economic Cooperation and Development. *Agricultural Policy in Japan*. Paris: Organization for Economic Cooperation and Development, 1974.

Pezeu-Massabuau, Jacques. *The Japanese Islands: A Physical and Social Geography*. Tokyo: Charles E. Tuttle Co., 1978.

Sanderson, Fred H. *Japan's Food Prospects and Policies* (Washington, D.C.: Brookings Institution, 1978).

Shimpo Mitsuru. *Three Decades in Shiwa: Economic Development and Social Change in a Japanese Farming Community*. Vancouver: University of British Columbia Press, 1976.

Singh, Rana P. B., and Yuihama Shōgo. *Changing Japanese Rural Habitat: Perspective and Prospect of the Agricultural Dimension*. New Delhi: National Geographic Society of India, 1981.

Smith, Robert J. *Kurusu: The Price of Progress in a Japanese Village, 1951-1975*. Stanford: Stanford University Press, 1978.

Smith, Thomas C. *The Agrarian Origins of Modern Japan*. Stanford: Stanford University Press, 1959.

Trewartha, Glenn T. *Japan: A Geography*. Madison: University of Wisconsin Press, 1965.

Tsuchiya Keizo. *Productivity and Technological Progress in Japanese Agriculture*. Tokyo: University of Tokyo Press, 1976.

Waswo, Ann. *Japanese Landlords: The Decline of a Rural Elite*. Berkeley: University of California Press, 1977.

Whitaker, Donald P. et al. *Japan: A Country Study*. Washington, D.C.: Department of the Army, 1983.

Yoshikawa Torao et al. *The Landforms of Japan*. Tokyo: University of Tokyo Press, 1981.

Articles in English

Akino M. "Land Infrastructure Improvement in Agricultural Development: The Japanese Case, 1900 to 1965." *Economic Development and Cultural Change* 28, no. 1 (October 1979): 97-111.

Bedford, Yukiko. "Grassroots Modernization in a Japanese Village." *Geojournal* 4, no. 3 (1980): 259-66.

Bromley, Daniel W.; Taylor, Donald C.; and Parker, Donald E. "Water Reform and Economic Development: Institutional Aspects of Water Management in Developing Countries." *Economic Development and Cultural Change* 28, no. 2 (January 1980): 365-87.

Brown, Keith. "Agriculture in Japan: The Crisis of Success." *Japan Society Newsletter* (Sept. 1986): 2-5.

Cornell, John B. Review of *Technology and Agricultural Development in Pre-War Japan*, by Penelope Francks, *Journal of Asian History* 20, no. 1 (1986): 111-13.

Coward, E. Walter, Jr. "Indigenous Institutions and Irrigation Development in Southeast Asia: Current Knowledge and Needed Research." In *Farm Water Management for Rice Cultivation*, pp. 113-30. Tokyo: Asian Productivity Organization, 1977.

_____. "Research Methodology in the Study of Irrigation Organization: A Review of Approaches and Applications." New York: Agricultural Development Council, 1978, no. 18.

Crawcour, E. "Japan 1869-1920." In *Agricultural Development in Asia*, edited by R. Shand, pp. 1-24. Canberra: Australian National University Press, 1969.

Donnelly, Michael W. "Setting the Price of Rice: A Study in Political Decision Making." In *Policymaking in Contemporary Japan*, edited by T. J. Pempel, pp. 143-200. Ithaca: Cornell University Press, 1977.

_____. "The Future of Japanese Agriculture." (Review article). *Pacific Affairs* 53, no. 4 (Winter 1980-81): 708-16.

_____. "Conflict over Government Authority and Markets: Japan's Rice Economy." In *Conflict in Japan*, edited by Ellis Krauss, Thomas P. Rohlen, and Patricia G. Steinhoff, pp. 355-74. Honolulu: University of Hawaii Press, 1984.

Dore, Ronald P. "Agricultural Improvement in Japan." *Economic Development and Cultural Change* 9, no. 1, pt. 2 (October 1960): 69-91.

Ebato Akira and Matsumura Norio. "Changes in Fruit Production in Japan." In *Geography of Japan*, edited by the Association of Japanese Geographers, Special Publication no. 4, pp. 223-45. Tokyo: Teikoku-Shoin Co., , 1980.

Egaitsu Fumio. "Japanese Agricultural Policy." In *U.S.-Japanese Agricultural Trade Relations*, edited by Emery Castle and Kenzō Hemmi, pp. 148-81. Baltimore: Johns Hopkins University Press, 1982.

Eyre, John D. "Water Controls in a Japanese Irrigation System." *Geographical Review* 45, no. 2 (April 1955): 197-216.

Freeman, David M. and Lowdermilk, Max K. "Middle-level Organizational Linkages in Irrigation Projects." In *Putting People First: Sociological Variables in Rural Development*, edited by Michael M. Cernea, pp. 52-90. New York: Oxford University Press, 1985.

George, Aurelia D. "The Japanese Farm Lobby and Agricultural Policy Making." *Pacific Affairs* 54, no. 3 (Fall 1981): 409-33.

Ginsburg, Norton. "The Regional Concept and Planning Regions." *Housing, Building and Planning*, nos. 12 and 13, pp. 31-45. New York: United Nations Department of Economic and Social Affairs, 1959-60.

_____. "Economic and Cultural Geography." In *An Introduction to Japanese Civilization*, edited by Arthur E. Tiedemann, pp. 423-59. New York: Columbia University Press, 1974.

Harris, Chauncy D. "The Urban and Industrial Transformation of Japan." *Geographical Review* 72, no. 1 (January 1982): 50-89.

Hayami Yūjirō. "Adjustment Policies for Japanese Agriculture in a Changing World." In *U.S.-Japanese Agricultural Trade Relations*, edited by

Emery Castle and Kenzō Hemmi, pp. 368-92. Baltimore: Johns Hopkins University Press, 1982.

Hemmi Kenzō. "Agriculture and Politics in Japan." In *U.S.-Japanese Agricultural Trade Relations*, edited by Emery Castle and Kenzō Hemmi, pp. 219-74. Baltimore: Johns Hopkins University Press, 1982.

Houck, James P. "Agreements and Policy in U.S.-Japanese Agricultural Trade." In *U.S.-Japanese Agricultural Trade Relations*, edited by Emery Castle and Kenzō Hemmi, pp. 58-87. Baltimore: Johns Hopkins University Press, 1982.

Ishii Motosuke. "Regional Trends in the Changing Agrarian Structure of Postwar Japan." In *Geography of Japan*, edited by the Association of Japanese Geographers, Special Publication no. 4., pp. 194-222. Tokyo: Teikoku-Shoin Co., 1980.

Ishimitsu Kenji and Gotō Junko. "Changing Rural Areas as the Object of Rural Planning in Japan." *Journal of Irrigation Engineering and Rural Planning*, no. 2 (July 1982): 28-42.

Itasaka, Gen, ed. *Encyclopedia of Japan* 1, s.v. "Agriculture." Tokyo: Kodansha Publishing Co., 1983.

Kanazawa Natsuki. "Role of Government and Farmers in Irrigation Water Utilization and Management." In *Farm Water Management and Rice Cultivation*, pp. 17-36. Tokyo: Asian Productivity Organization, 1977.

Kimura Takashige. "Japan--1." In *Farm Water Management for Rice Cultivation*, pp. 248-66. Tokyo: Asian Productivity Organization, 1977.

Kornhauser, David H. Review of *Water Control in Tokugawa Japan: Irrigation Organization in a Japanese River Basin* and *Irrigation Management in Japan: A Critical Review of Japanese Social Science Research*, by William W. Kelly. In *Monumentica Nipponica* 37, no. 4 (1985): 465-66.

Kuroda Yoshimi. "The Present State of Agriculture in Japan." In *U.S.-Japanese Agricultural Trade Relations*, edited by Emery Castle and Kenzō Hemmi, pp. 91-147. Baltimore: Johns Hopkins University Press, 1982.

Latz, Gil. "Agricultural Adjustments in Japan." *Center News* (Japanese Studies Center--Japan Foundation) 8, no. 2 (June 1983): 2-4. (Review of public lecture by Professor Hemmi Kenzō, April 20, 1983.)

_____. "Agricultural Infrastructure Development in Japan: The Case of Saitama Prefecture and the Minuma Land Improvement District." In *Proceedings: Research Exchange Symposium between Hokkaidō University and Portland State University, July 10-12, 1986,* edited by Executive Committee for Research Exchange Symposium between Hokkaidō University and Portland State University, pp. 1-66 (Sapporo, Japan: Hokkaidō University, 1987).

_____. "The Persistence of Agricultural Activity in Urban Japan: An Analysis of the Tokyo Metropolitan Area," in *The Extended Metropolis in Asia,* edited by Norton Ginsburg and T. G. McGee (Honolulu: University of Hawaii Press, in press).

Nishikawa Osamu. "Land Improvement and Modernization of Rural Areas in Japan." *Proceedings,* Department of the Humanities, College of General Education, University of Tokyo, Series on Human Geography 52, 1971: 13-36.

_____. "Land Improvement in Relation to Landforms." *Proceedings,* Department of the Humanities, College of General Education, University of Tokyo, Series on Human Geography 56, 1973: 1-20.

Nishikawa Osamu and Latz, Gil. "The Role of Land Improvement Districts (*Tochi Kairyō Ku*) in the Modernization of Japan's Agricultural Sector: A Preliminary Research Report." *Proceedings,* Department of the Humanities, College of General Education, University of Tokyo 73, Series on Human Geography no. 7 (March 1981): 53-70.

Ogasawara Yoshikatsu. "The Role of Rice and Rice Paddy [*sic*] Development in Japan." *Bulletin of the Geographical Survey Institute* 5, pt. 4 (March 1958): 1-23.

Okita Saburō. "The Proper Approach to Food Policy." *Japan Echo* 5, no. 2 (Summer 1978): 49-57.

Ravenholt, Albert. "The Japanese Farmer: Wheat or Rice for the Yen?" *American Universities Field Staff Reports,* Asia, 1978, no. 18.

Ruttan, Vernon W. "Induced Institutional Change." In *Induced Innovation: Technology, Institutions and Development*, edited by Hans Binswanger and Vernon Ruttan, pp. 327-57. Baltimore: Johns Hopkins University Press, 1978.

Sanderson, Fred. H. "Managing Our Agricultural Interdependence." In *U.S.-Japanese Agricultural Trade Relations*, edited by Emery Castle and Kenzō Hemmi, pp. 393-426. Baltimore: Johns Hopkins University Press, 1982.

Sawada S. "The Development of Rice Productivity in Japan: Pre-War Experience." In *Agriculture and Economic Development*, edited by Japan Economic Research Center, pp. 115-40. Tokyo: Japan Economic Research Center, 1972.

Senga Yūtarō and Shimura Hiroyasu. "Study of Methods for Estimation of Water Resources Development Stages." *Journal of Irrigation Engineering and Rural Planning*, no. 2 (July 1982): 6-16.

Shanmugaratnam, Nadarajah. "Symptoms of Structural Crisis: A Visit to a Japanese Paddy Village." In *Toward Structural Reform of Japanese Agriculture*, edited by Takekazu Ogura, pp. 29-58. Tokyo: Agricultural Policy Research Center, 1983.

Singh, Rana P. B. and Yuihama Shōgo. "Recent Structural Transformation of Japanese Agriculture: National Perspective and Vision of Okayama-ken." In *Environmental Appraisal and Rural Habitat Transformation*, edited by R. L. Singh, pp. 203-27. NGSI Pub. 32, IGC Paris vol. 25, 1984.

Spencer, J. E. "Water Control in Terraced Rice Field Agriculture in Southeastern Asia." In *Irrigation's Impact on Society*, edited by Thomas E. Downing and M. Gibson, pp. 59-65. Tucson: University of Arizona Press, Anthropological Paper no. 25, 1974.

Tamaki Akira. "Development of Local Culture and the Irrigation System of the Azusa Basin." Tokyo: United Nations University, Projects on Technology, Transfer, Transformation, and Development: The Japanese Experience (HSDRJE-4/UNUP-50), 1979.

VanderMeer, Canute. "Water Thievery in a Rice Irrigation System in Taiwan." *Annals of the Association of American Geographers* 61 (March 1971): 156-79.

_____. "Changing Local Patterns in a Taiwanese Irrigation System." In *Irrigation and Agricultural Development in Asia,* edited by E. Walter Coward, Jr., pp. 225-62. Ithaca: Cornell University Press, 1980.

Whitney, Joseph. "East Asia." In *World Systems of Traditional Resource Management and Conservation,* edited by Gary A. Klee, pp. 101-29. London: Edward Arnold, 1980.

Bulletins and Pamphlets in English

Association for Asian Studies. Program of the Thirty-Seventh Annual Meeting, 1985. "Japanese Agriculture: The Crisis of Family Farming and Structural Reform," chaired by John B. Cornell.

_____. Program of the Thirty-Ninth Annual Meeting, 1987. "High Tech and 'High Touch,' Part One: The Meanings of Technology."

Coyle, William T. *Japan's Rice Policy.* Washington, D.C.: United States Department of Agriculture, Economic and Statistics Service, Foreign Agricultural Economic Report 164, 1981.

Japan, Ministry of Foreign Affairs. "Facts about Japan: Agriculture." Tokyo: Public Information Bureau, 1977.

Japan, National Land Agency. "Water Resources Policy in Japan." Tokyo: National Land Agency, National Land Policy Series no. 3, 1977.

Japan, Water Resources Bureau, National Land Agency. "Water Resources in Japan." Tokyo: National Land Agency, Water Resources Bureau, 1977.

Kalmbach, Paul M.; Sharp, John W.; and Walker, Francis E. "The Japanese Food and Feed Grain Economy." Wooster, Ohio: Ohio Agricultural Research and Development Center, *Research Bulletin* 1126, 1981.

United States-Japan Trade Council. "U.S.-Japan Agricultural Trade: What's Ahead in the 1980s." Washington, D.C.: United States-Japan Trade Council, 1979.

Unpublished Sources in English

Cornell, John B. "Urban Villagers or Post-Industrial Peasant?: The Impact of Public Policy on Family Farming in a Japanese Mountain Village." Paper presented at the 1985 meetings of the Association for Asian Studies, Philadelphia, March 22, 1985.

Latz, Gil. "Accelerated Soil Erosion and the Implementation of Conservation Techniques: The Black Creek Project, Allen County, Indiana." Master's Paper, Department of Geography, University of Chicago, 1978.

_____. "Preparatory Research for a Comparison of Agricultural Water Resource Management Policy Concepts and Practice in Japan and the United States" [*Nihon to amerika ni okeru nōgyō mizu shigen seisaku no rinen to jissai no hikaku kenkyū' ni kan suru yobiteki kenkyū*]. Toyota Foundation, National Grant 80-1-192, 1981-82.

_____. "Preparatory Research for a Comparison of Agricultural Water Resource Management Policy Concepts and Practice in Japan and the United States" [*Nihon to amerika ni okeru nōgyō mizu shigen seisaku no rinen to jissai no hikaku kenkyū' ni kan suru yobiteki kenkyū*]. Toyota Foundation, National Grant 82-S-007, 1983.

_____. "Preparatory Research for Publication of Agricultural Water Resource Management Policy Concepts and Practice in Japan." Toyota Foundation, National Grant 84-S-001, 1985.

Senga Yūtarō. "Water Requirements for Farming: Water Rights and Water Resources." Photocopy. 1980.

Takahashi Yutaka. "Changes and Processes of Water Resource Development and Flood Control in post-WWII Japan." Photocopy. 1982.

United States Embassy, Tokyo, Japan. "Attache Reports." Foreign Agricultural Service, United States Department of Agriculture, 1980-83. Photocopies.

Vaidyanathan, A. "Kansai Field Trip: Impressions." Photocopy. August 1982.

Yuihama Shōgo. "An Outline of Problems of Paddy Field Agriculture in Japan." Photocopy. 1981.

Interviews/Field Trips: 1980-84

Iwamura Yasuyuki, Ebara Corporation, Tokyo, January 1980 (multiple interviews conducted through 1984).

Thomas L. Blakemore, lawyer, Blakemore and Mitsuki, Tokyo, January 1980 (multiple interviews conducted through 1984).

Yamaguchi Takashi, professor, Institute of Human Geography, University of Tokyo, February 1980 (multiple interviews conducted through 1984).

Nishikawa Osamu, professor and chairman, Institute of Human Geography, University of Tokyo, April 1980 (multiple interviews conducted through 1984).

Tanabe Hiroshi, professor, Institute of Human Geography, University of Tokyo, April 1980 (multiple interviews conducted through 1984).

Kobori Iwao, associate professor, Geography Department, University of Tokyo, April 1980 (multiple interviews conducted through 1982).

Takahashi Akira, professor, Economics Department, University of Tokyo, April 1980 (multiple interviews conducted through 1983).

Shimura Hiroyasu, professor, Laboratory of Irrigation and Drainage, Faculty of Agriculture, University of Tokyo, April 1980 (multiple interviews conducted through 1983).

Nakamura Ryōta, associate professor, Laboratory of Irrigation and Drainage, Faculty of Agriculture, University of Tokyo, April 1980 (multiple interviews conducted through 1983).

Takahashi Yutaka, professor, Department of Civil Engineering, University of Tokyo; April 1980 (multiple interviews conducted through 1983).

Senga Yūtarō, associate professor, Department of Rural Engineering, Utsunomiya University, May 1980 (multiple interviews conducted through 1983).

Mizutani Masakazu, associate professor, Department of Agriculture, Mie University, May 1980 (multiple interviews conducted through 1983).

Arai Yoshio, associate professor, Faculty of Economics, Shinshū University, May 1980 (multiple interviews conducted through 1983).

Satō Tetsuo, research associate, Institute of Human Geography, University of Tokyo, May 1980 (multiple interviews conducted through 1983).

Naitō Masanori, research associate, Institute of Human Geography, University of Tokyo, May 1980 (multiple interviews conducted through 1983).

Shibusawa Masahide, Tokyo, May 1980 (multiple interviews conducted through 1983).

Itō Michio, senior program officer, Japan Center for International Exchange, Tokyo, May 1980 (multiple interviews conducted through 1982).

Justin Bloom, counselor for scientific and technological affairs, United States Embassy in Tokyo, August 1980.

Isawa Senjōchi field trip, Iwate prefecture, August 1980 (accompanied by Satō Tetsuo, research associate, University of Tokyo).

Yatsushiro Tochi Kairyō Ku Jimusho, Kumamoto prefecture, December 1980 (accompanied by Satō Tetsuo, research associate, University of Tokyo).

Tamanoi Yoshio, professor, Department of Economics, Okinawa Gakuin University, December 1980.

Nōrinsuisanshō Kōzōkaizenkyoku, Tokyo, May 1981 (multiple interviews conducted through 1983).

Yamada Harumichi, graduate student, Institute of Human Geography, University of Tokyo, June 1981 (multiple interviews conducted through 1982).

Hemmi Kenzō, professor, Department of Agricultural Economics, University of Tokyo, June 1981 (in conjunction with participation as an observer in the Conference on Bypassed Economic Areas in Asian Economic Development, in Naha, Okinawa).

Okamoto Masami, professor, Department of Civil Engineering and Land Planning, Iwate University, June 1981 (multiple interviews conducted through 1982).

Nakanojō Tochi Kairyō Ku Jimusho, Gunma prefecture, July 1981 (field trip led by Professor Yamaguchi Takashi, University of Tokyo).

Nagano Kenchō and Ina Tochi Kairyō Ku Jimusho, Nagano prefecture, August 1981 (field trip led by Professor Nishikawa Osamu, University of Tokyo).

Nishikanbara Tochi Kairyō Ku Jimusho, Niigata prefecture, September 1981 (accompanied by Mr. Yamada Harumichi, graduate student, University of Tokyo).

Ouji Toshiaki, associate professor, Department of Geography, Kyoto University, October 1981 (interview and local field trip).

Takaya Yoshikazu, professor, Center for Southeast Asian Studies, Kyoto University, October 1981.

Shibata Kyōhei, associate professor, Faculty of Economics, Shinshū University, December 1981 (multiple interviews conducted through 1984).

Minuma Tochi Kairyō Ku Jimusho, Saitama Prefecture, April 1982 (field trip led by Professor Nishikawa Osamu, University of Tokyo).

Yamamoto Shigeo, assistant section chief, Kōchi Keikaku Ka, Nōrinbu, Saitama prefecture, April 1982 (multiple interviews conducted through 1983).

Ina Yoshihiko, head, Saitama Ken Nōrinbu, Kōchika, Saitama prefecture, April 1982 (multiple interviews conducted through 1983).

Wada Hiroshi, chief of the administrative section, Minuma Tochi Kairyō Ku Jimusho, April 1982 (multiple interviews conducted through 1983).

Gotō Junko, researcher, Rural Development and Planning Commission, May 1982 (multiple interviews conducted through 1983).

Suzanne Hale, agricultural attaché, United States Embassy in Tokyo, July 1982 (multiple interviews conducted through 1984).

Sayama Ike Tochi Kairyō Ku Jimusho, Kōmyō Ike Tochi Kairyō Ku Jimusho, and Kotsu Tochi Kairyō Ku Jimusho (Osaka-fu and Gifu prefecture), August 1982 (field trip led by Professor Okamoto Masami, Iwate University).

Nakamura Hisashi, researcher, Institute of Developing Economies, Tokyo, August 1982.

A. Vaidynathan, visiting researcher, Institute of Developing Economies, Tokyo, August 1982.

Nadarajah Shanmugaratnam, visiting researcher, Institute of Developing Economies, Tokyo, August 1982.

Endō Hiroshi, researcher, Okurasho, Tokyo, September 1982.

Yuihama Shōgo, professor, Geography Department, Okayama University, October 1982 (in conjunction with field trip to Kojima Wan Tochi Kairyō Ku Jimusho, Okayama City).

Moritaki Kenichirō, professor, Geography Department, Okayama University, October 1982 (interview and field trip to Kojima Wan Tochi Kairyō Ku Jimusho, Okayama City).

Niike Tochi Kairyō Ku Jimusho, Okayama prefecture, October 1982 (field trip arranged by Professor Okamoto Masami, and led by Doi Hiroshi, Okayama prefecture).

Shirai Yoshihiko, professor, Hyōgo University of Teacher Education, October 1982 (interview and field trip in Hyogo prefecture).

Saitama prefecture, Minumadai irrigation canal, December 1982 (field trip led by Associate Professor Mizutani Masakazu, Mie University).

Takahara Susumu, secretariat, Nōgyō Doboku Gakkai, Tokyo, February 1983.

Sano Tochi Kairyō Ku, Tochigi prefecture, April 1983 (field trip led by Associate Professor Senga Yūtarō, Utsunomiya University).

Miyazaki Kenchō, Miyazaki prefecture, May 1983 (field trip led by Associate Professor Senga Yūtarō, Utsunomiya University).

Suwa Nōgyō Kyōdō Kumiai Jimusho, Nagano prefecture, July 1983 (field trip led by Associate Professors Arai Yoshio and Shibata Kyohei, Shinshū University).

Hanayama Yuzuru, professor, Department of Social Engineering, Japan Institute of Technology, Tokyo, July 1983.

Kōzuma Naomasa, executive director, Toshi Keizai Kenkyū Jo, Tokyo, October 1983 (multiple interviews, summer 1984).

Nishioka Hisao, president and professor, Aoyama Gakuin University, Tokyo, June 1986.

Tominomori Kenji, professor, Faculty of Economics, Hokkaidō University, summer 1986.

INDEX

Adachi-*ku*, 74
Administrative terminology. *See* Agriculture
Agricultural Basic Law, 49, 64, 65n, 72, 93
Agricultural civil engineering technology. *See* Canal; Agricultural infrastructure, consolidation
Agricultural Cooperative Association, 14, 15n, 46n
(Agricultural Cooperative) Association Financing, 46n
Agricultural development: process of, 1; features of, 9-10; relation to technology, 14. *See also* Land improvement
Agricultural frontier, 12, 23
Agricultural infrastructure: definition of, 1; consolidation, 45n, 49, 62; contrasted to agricultural structure improvement projects, 50n; Saitama prefecture costs for, 66n. *See* Agricultural structure improvement
Agricultural land consolidation, 66n
Agricultural land development, 37n
Agricultural Land Law, 35
Agricultural landscape. *See* Agriculture
Agricultural research, 14
Agricultural structure improvement: policy for, 1; projects for, 50; contrasted to agricultural infrastructure consolidation, 50n
Agricultural trade, 14, 15n. *See also* Agriculture; Self-sufficiency
Agricultural water-use rationalization, 40, 60, 73; relation to land improvement in Saitama prefecture, 64; definition of projects for, 64n; characteristics of projects in Minuma LID, 83-85; use of technology to promote agricultural water use, 84-85; water leakage preventing technology, 84n, 85n; history in Saitama prefecture, 84n
Agriculture: characteristics of, 2n, 6n, 17-18, 20, 21n, 24, 33n, 41-45, 91; policy for, 1, 7-8,15n, 32, 35-36, 55, 91; administrative terminology for, 5, 7, 13, 89-90, 93; self-

sufficiency, 15n,18; relation to imports, 31-32; labor force, 23n; yield, 24, 29-30; tenancy, 25; depopulation of, 26-27; development problems associated with, 41-45; land price, 28; twentieth-century changes in, 33-34; suburbanization and industrialization of, 15-16, 78-85, 93, 95. *See also* Canal; Irrigation; Land improvement; Wet paddy; Dry field; Financing
Agriculture, Forestry and Fisheries: Ministry of, 81; Financing Corporation, 46n, 63n; relation to functions of LID, 92n
Alluvial lowlands, 18; definition of, 20
Ara River, 74, 83n, 85n
Arable land: amount of, 12, 17-18, 23; soils, 20
Arable Land Reorganization: Law, 38-40, 53; Association, 11, 38, 39n; in comparison to Regular Water-Use Associations, 39n
Are: definition of, 37n, 42n, 44; national pattern, 44-45; pattern in Saitama prefecture, 70-72. *See* Farmland consolidation; Land readjustment
Associations or Organizations. *See* Agricultural Cooperative Association; Arable Land Reorganization Association; Arable Land Reorganization Law; (Agricultural Cooperative) Association Financing; Land Improvement District; Land Improvement, Law; Ordinance for Water-Use Associations; Regular Water-Use Association; Regular Water-Use Association Law

Baiu (early summer rainy season), 20
Bakufu, 74n
Benefited area: definition of, 79-80, 95; Minumadai irrigation canal characteristics, 80-87
Branch (sub-main) drainage canal, 37n
Branch (sub-main) irrigation canal,37n
Buddhism, 22

Water bridge, 75n
Water control. *See* Irrigation and drainage
    canal maintenance; Agricultural water-use
    rationalization
Water depth requirement, 21n
Water Resources Development Promotion
    Law, 64-65, 73
Water Resources Development Public
    Corporation, 64n
Water use. *See* Regular Water-Use
    Association; Regular Water-Use
    Association Law; Ordinance for Water-
    Use Associations; Customary water-use
    practices; Agricultural water-use
    rationalization, projects
Water valve, spigot-type, 44
Water warming canal, 37n; facilities, 36,
    37n; ponds, 37n
Weir, 7n, 36, 37n (including dams,
    headworks, canals and irrigation
    networks). *See also* Diversion weir; Fixed
    weir; Movable weir; Slanted weir
Well, relief (modern), 44n
Wet-field agriculture, 6n, 7
Wet-paddy: definition of, 2n, 6n, 7, 21;
    distribution of, 18, 30; history of, 22; basis
    of traditional fiscal system, 22; yield, 24,
    30; total production of, 29-30, 32; demand
    for, 31-32; diversification away from, 32-
    33; production characteristics, 41-42. *See
    also* Agriculture; Land improvement

THE UNIVERSITY OF CHICAGO
GEOGRAPHY RESEARCH PAPERS
(Lithographed, 6 x 9 inches)

Titles in Print

120. MIHELIC, DUESAN. *The Political Element in the Port Geography of Trieste.* 1969. ix + 104 p.

121. BAUMANN, DUANE D. *The Recreational Use of Domestic Water Supply Reservoirs: Perception and Choice.* 1969. ix + 125 p.

122. LIND, AULIS O. *Coastal Landforms of Cat Island, Bahamas: A Study of Holocene Accretionary Topography and Sea-Level Change.* 1969. ix + 156 p.

123. WHITNEY, JOSEPH B. R. *China: Area, Administration and Nation Building.* 1970. xiii + 198 p.

124. EARICKSON, ROBERT. *The Spatial Behavior of Hospital Patients: A Behavioral Approach to Spatial Interaction in Metropolitan Chicago.* 1970. xi + 138 p.

125. DAY, JOHN C. *Managing the Lower Rio Grande: An Experience in International River Development.* 1970. xii + 274 p.

126. MacIVER, IAN. *Urban Water Supply Alternatives: Perception and Choice in the Grand Basin, Ontario.* 1970. ix + 178 p.

127. GOHEEN, PETER G. *Victorian Toronto, 1850 to 1900: Pattern and Process of Growth.* 1970. xiii + 278 p.

128. GOOD, CHARLES M. *Rural Markets and Trade in East Africa.* 1970. xvi + 252 p.

129. MEYER, DAVID R. *Spatial Variation of Black Urban Households.* 1970. xiv + 127 p.

130. GLADFELTER, BRUCE G. *Meseta and Campina Landforms in Central Spain: A Geomorphology of the Alto Henares Basin.* 1971. xii + 204 p.

131. NEILS, ELAINE M. *Reservation to City: Indian Migration and Federal Relocation.* 1971. x + 198 p.

132. MOLINE, NORMAN T. *Mobility and the Small Town, 1900-1930.* 1971. ix + 169 p.

133. SCHWIND, PAUL J. *Migration and Regional Development in the United States, 1950-1960.* 1971. x + 170 p.

134. PYLE, GERALD F. *Heart Disease, Cancer and Stroke in Chicago: A Geographical Analysis with Facilities, Plans for 1980.* 1971. ix + 292 p.

135. JOHNSON, JAMES F. *Renovated Waste Water: An Alternative Source of Municipal Water Supply in the United States.* 1971. ix + 155 p.

136. BUTZER, KARL W. *Recent History of an Ethiopian Delta: The Omo River and the Level of Lake Rudolf.* 1971. xvi + 184 p.

139. McMANIS, DOUGLAS R. *European Impressions of the New England Coast, 1497-1620.* 1972. viii + 147 p.

140. COHEN, YEHOSHUA S. *Diffusion of an Innovation in an Urban System: The Spread of Planned Regional Shopping Centers in the United States, 1949-1968.* 1972. ix + 136 p.

141. MITCHELL, NORA. *The Indian Hill-Station: Kodaikanal.* 1972. xii + 199 p.

142. PLATT, RUTHERFORD H. *The Open Space Decision Process: Spatial Allocation of Costs and Benefits.* 1972. xi + 189 p.

143. GOLANT, STEPHEN M. *The Residential Location and Spatial Behavior of the Elderly: A Canadian Example.* 1972. xv + 226 p.

144. PANNELL, CLIFTON W. *T'ai-Chung, T'ai-wan: Structure and Function.* 1973. xii + 200 p.

145. LANKFORD, PHILIP M. *Regional Incomes in the United States, 1929-1967: Level, Distribution, Stability, and Growth.* 1972. x + 137 p.

146. FREEMAN, DONALD B. *International Trade, Migration, and Capital Flows: A Quantitative Analysis of Spatial Economic Interaction.* 1973. xiv + 201 p.

147. MYERS, SARAH K. *Language Shift among Migrants to Lima, Peru.* 1973. xiii + 203 p.

148. JOHNSON, DOUGLAS L. *Jabal al-Akhdar, Cyrenaica: An Historical Geography of Settlement and Livelihood.* 1973. xii + 240 p.

149. YEUNG, YUE-MAN. *National Development Policy and Urban Transformation in Singapore: A Study of Public Housing and the Marketing System.* 1973. x + 204 p.

150. HALL, FRED L. *Location Criteria for High Schools: Student Transportation and Racial Integration.* 1973. xii + 156 p.

151. ROSENBERG, TERRY J. *Residence, Employment, and Mobility of Puerto Ricans in New York City.* 1974. xi + 230 p.

152. MIKESELL, MARVIN W., ed. *Geographers Abroad: Essays on the Problems and Prospects of Research in Foreign Areas.* 1973. ix + 296 p.

153. OSBORN, JAMES. *Area, Development Policy, and the Middle City in Malaysia.* 1974. x+ 291 p.

154. WACHT, WALTER F. *The Domestic Air Transportation Network of the United States.* 1974. ix + 98 p.

155. BERRY, BRIAN J. L. et al. *Land Use, Urban Form and Environmental Quality.* 1974. xxiii + 440 p.

156. MITCHELL, JAMES K. *Community Response to Coastal Erosion: Individual and Collective Adjustments to Hazard on the Atlantic Shore.* 1974. xii + 209 p.

157. COOK, GILLIAN P. *Spatial Dynamics of Business Growth in the Witwatersrand.* 1975. x + 144 p.

159. PYLE, GERALD F. et al. *The Spatial Dynamics of Crime.* 1974. x + 221 p.

160. MEYER, JUDITH W. *Diffusion of an American Montessori Education.* 1975. xi + 97 p.

161. SCHMID, JAMES A. *Urban Vegetation: A Review and Chicago Case Study.* 1975. xii + 266 p.

162. LAMB, RICHARD F. *Metropolitan Impacts on Rural America.* 1975. xii + 196 p.

163. FEDOR, THOMAS STANLEY. *Patterns of Urban Growth in the Russian Empire during the Nineteenth Century.* 1975. xxv + 245 p.

164. HARRIS, CHAUNCY D. *Guide to Geographical Bibliographies and Reference Works in Russian or on the Soviet Union.* 1975. xviii + 478 p.

165. JONES, DONALD W. *Migration and Urban Unemployment in Dualistic Economic Development.* 1975. x + 174 p.

166. BEDNARZ, ROBERT S. *The Effect of Air Pollution on Property Value in Chicago.* 1975. viii + 111 p.

167. HANNEMANN, MANFRED. *The Diffusion of the Reformation in Southwestern Germany, 1518-1534.* 1975. ix + 235 p.

168. SUBLETT, MICHAEL D. *Farmers on the Road: Interfarm Migration and the Farming of Noncontiguous Lands in Three Midwestern Townships. 1939-1969.* 1975. xiii + 214 p.

169. STETZER, DONALD FOSTER. *Special Districts in Cook County: Toward a Geography of Local Government.* 1975. xi + 177 p.

171. SPODEK, HOWARD. *Urban-Rural Integration in Regional Development: A Case Study of Saurashtra, India—1800-1960.* 1976. xi + 144 p.

172. COHEN, YEHOSHUA S., and BRIAN J. L. BERRY. *Spatial Components of Manufacturing Change.* 1975. vi + 262 p.

173. HAYES, CHARLES R. *The Dispersed City: The Case of Piedmont, North Carolina.* 1976. ix + 157 p.

174. CARGO, DOUGLAS B. *Solid Wastes: Factors Influencing Generation Rates.* 1977. viii + 100 p.

175. GILLARD, QUENTIN. *Incomes and Accessibility: Metropolitan Labor Force Partici-pation, Commuting, and Income Differentials in the United States, 1960-1970.* 1977. ix + 106 p.

176. MORGAN, DAVID J. *Patterns of Population Distribution: A Residential Preference Model and Its Dynamic.* 1978. xiii + 200 p.

177. STOKES, HOUSTON H., DONALD W. JONES, AND HUGH M. NEUBURGER. *Unemployment and Adjustment in the Labor Market: A Comparison between the Regional and National Responses.* 1975. ix + 125 p.

180. CARR, CLAUDIA J. *Pastoralism in Crisis. The Dasanetch and Their Ethiopian Lands.* 1977. xx + 319 p.

181. GOODWIN, GARY C. *Cherokees in Transition: A Study of Changing Culture and Environment Prior to 1775.* 1977. ix + 207 p.

182. KNIGHT, DAVID B. *A Capital for Canada: Conflict and Compromise in the Nine-teenth Century.* 1977. xvii + 341 p.

183. HAIGH, MARTIN J. *The Evolution of Slopes on Artificial Landforms, Blaenavon, U.K.* 1978. xiv + 293 p.

184. FINK, L. DEE. *Listening to the Learner: An Exploratory Study of Personal Meaning in College Geography Courses.* 1977. ix + 186 p.

185. HELGREN, DAVID M. *Rivers of Diamonds: An Alluvial History of the Lower Vaal Basin, South Africa.* 1979. xix + 389 p.

186. BUTZER, KARL W., ed. *Dimensions of Human Geography: Essays on Some Familiar and Neglected Themes.* 1978. vii + 190 p.

187. MITSUHASHI, SETSUKO. *Japanese Commodity Flows.* 1978. x + 172 p.

188. CARIS, SUSAN L. *Community Attitudes toward Pollution.* 1978. xii + 211 p.

189. REES, PHILIP M. *Residential Patterns in American Cities: 1960.* 1979. xvi + 405 p.

190. KANNE, EDWARD A. *Fresh Food for Nicosia.* 1979. x + 106 p.

192. KIRCHNER, JOHN A. *Sugar and Seasonal Labor Migration: The Case of Tucumán, Argentina.* 1980. xii + 174 p.

193. HARRIS, CHAUNCY D., AND JEROME D. FELLMANN. *International List of Geographical Serials, Third Edition, 1980.* 1980. vi + 457 p.

194. HARRIS, CHAUNCY D. *Annotated World List of Selected Current Geographical Serials, Fourth Edition. 1980.* 1980. iv + 165 p.

195. LEUNG, CHI-KEUNG. *China: Railway Patterns and National Goals.* 1980. xv + 243 p.

196. LEUNG, CHI-KEUNG, AND NORTON S. GINSBURG, eds. *China: Urbanizations and National Development.* 1980. ix + 283 p.

197. DAICHES, SOL. *People in Distress: A Geographical Perspective on Psychological Well-being.* 1981. xiv + 199 p.

198. JOHNSON, JOSEPH T. *Location and Trade Theory: Industrial Location, Comparative Advantage, and the Geographic Pattern of Production in the United States.* 1981. xi + 107 p.

199-200. STEVENSON, ARTHUR J. *The New York-Newark Air Freight System.* 1982. xvi + 440 p.

201. LICATE, JACK A. *Creation of a Mexican Landscape: Territorial Organization and Settlement in the Eastern Puebla Basin, 1520-1605.* 1981. x + 143 p.

202. RUDZITIS, GUNDARS. *Residential Location Determinants of the Older Population.* 1982. x + 117 p.

203. LIANG, ERNEST P. *China: Railways and Agricultural Development, 1875-1935.* 1982. xi + 186 p.

204. DAHMANN, DONALD C. *Locals and Cosmopolitans: Patterns of Spatial Mobility during the Transition from Youth to Early Adulthood.* 1982. xiii + 146 p.

205. FOOTE, KENNETH E. *Color in Public Spaces: Toward a Communication-Bases Theory of the Urban Built Environment.* 1983. xiv + 153 p.

206. HARRIS, CHAUNCY D. *Bibliography of Geography. Part II: Regional. Volume 1. The United States of America.* 1984. viii + 178 p.

207-208. WHEATLEY, PAUL. *Nagara and Commandery: Origins of the Southeast Asian Urban Traditions.* 1983. xv + 472 p.

209. SAARINEN, THOMAS F., DAVID SEAMON, AND JAMES L. SELL, eds. *Environmental Perception and Behavior: An Inventory and Prospect.* 1984. x + 263 p.

210. WESCOAT, JAMES L., JR. *Integrated Water Development: Water Use and Conservation Practice in Western Colorado.* 1984. xi + 239 p.

211. DEMKO, GEORGE J., AND ROLAND J. FUCHS, eds. *Geographical Studies on the Soviet Union: Essays in Honor of Chauncy D. Harris.* 1984. vii + 294 p.

212. HOLMES, ROLAND C. *Irrigation in Southern Peru: The Chili Basin.* 1986. ix + 199 p.

213. EDMONDS, RICHARD LOUIS. *Northern Frontiers of Qing China and Tokugawa Japan: A Comparative Study of Frontier Policy.* 1985. xi + 209 p.

214. FREEMAN, DONALD B., AND GLEN B. NORCLIFFE. *Rural Enterprise in Kenya: Development and Spatial Organization of the Nonfarm Sector.* 1985. xiv + 180 p.

215. COHEN, YEHOSHUA S., AND AMNON SHINAR. *Neighborhoods and Friendship Networks: A Study of Three Residential Neighborhoods in Jerusalem.* 1985. ix +137 p.

217-218. CONZEN, MICHAEL P., ed. *World Patterns of Modern Urban Change: Essays in Honor of Chauncy D. Harris.* 1986. x + 479 p.

219. KOMOGUCHI, YOSHIMI. *Agricultural Systems in the Tamil Nadu: A Case Study of Peruvalanallur Village.* 1986. xvi + 175 p.

220. GINSBURG, NORTON, JAMES OBORN, AND GRANT BLANK. *Geographic Perspectives on the Wealth of Nations.* 1986. ix + 1331 p.

221. BAYLSON, JOSHUA C. *Territorial Allocation by Imperial Rivalry: The Human Legacy in the Near East.* 1987. xi + 138 p.

224. PLATT, RUTHERFORD H., SHEILA G. PELCZARSKI, AND BARBARA K. BURBANK, eds. *Cities on the Beach: Management Issues of Developed Coastal Barriers.* 1987. vii + 324 p.

225. LATZ, GIL. *Agricultural Development in Japan: The Land Improvement District in Concept and Practice.* 1989. viii + 135 p.

226. GRITZNER, JEFFREY A. *The West African Sahel: Human Agency and Environmental Change.* 1988. xii + 170 p.

227. MURPHY, ALEXANDER B. *The Regional Dynamics of Language Differentiation in Belgium: A Study in Cultural-Political Geography.* 1988. xiii + 249 p.